The Swedish Corporate Bond Market

CHALLENGES AND POLICY RECOMMENDATIONS

OECD
BETTER POLICIES FOR BETTER LIVES

Please cite this publication as:
OECD (2024), *The Swedish Corporate Bond Market: Challenges and Policy Recommendations*, OECD Publishing, Paris, https://doi.org/10.1787/7ff1a6ce-en.

ISBN 978-92-64-93792-5 (print)
ISBN 978-92-64-62159-6 (PDF)
ISBN 978-92-64-47756-8 (HTML)
ISBN 978-92-64-85538-0 (epub)

Photo credits: Cover © Aliaksandr Antanovich/GettyImages.

Corrigenda to OECD publications may be found on line at: www.oecd.org/about/publishing/corrigenda.htm.

Foreword

Drawing from detailed empirical analysis, interviews and consultations with key institutions and market participants, this report provides an assessment of the Swedish non-financial corporate bond market and formulates policy recommendations to address current and future challenges.

The empirical overview, which is based on original data, offers an account of how the market has developed during the past two decades, documenting in particular changes since the 2008 financial crisis with respect to market size, credit quality and issuer and investor profile. These developments are also considered in an international context, comparing the Swedish market with those in other countries. This overview is based on an OECD mapping report published in October 2022 titled *The Swedish Corporate Bond Market and Bondholder Rights*.

The report has been prepared by the OECD in co-operation with the Swedish Corporate Governance Institute (SCGI). It is part of a broader SCGI project on Swedish capital markets, co-financed by the Nasdaq Nordic Foundation and Vinnova.

OECD CAPITAL MARKET SERIES

The report is part of the OECD Capital Market Series, which informs policy discussions on how capital markets can serve their important role of channelling financial resources from households to productive investments in the real economy.

Detailed descriptions of the data sources, selected indicators and the methodology for data collection and analysis are provided in the Annex. The report also draws from fact-finding missions and consultations with representatives of both government institutions and market participants, including the Swedish Riksbank, the Swedish Financial Supervisory Authority (*Finansinspektionen*), Nasdaq Stockholm, leading legal and financial advisors, banks, issuers, agents and stakeholder organisations. The report has benefitted greatly from these interviews and consultations, and the team gratefully acknowledges the participants' important contributions.

The report was prepared by a team from the OECD composed of Carl Magnus Magnusson and Alejandra Medina, led by Serdar Çelik, Head of the Capital Markets and Financial Institutions Division within the OECD Directorate for Financial and Enterprise Affairs, together with a team from the SCGI composed of Mats Isaksson, co-Director of the SCGI, and Erik Lidman, co-Director of the SCGI and Associate Professor at the Universities of Stockholm and Gothenburg.

Table of contents

FIGURES

TABLES

Acronyms and abbreviations

APA	Approved Publication Arrangement
ATS	Alternative Trading System
CTP	Consolidated Tape Provider
DC	Domestic Currency
ECB	European Central Bank
ESMA	European Securities and Markets Authority
ESRB	European Systemic Risk Board
EU	European Union
FI	*Finansinspektionen* (Swedish FSA)
FIBEN	*Fichier bancaire des entreprises*
FINRA	Financial Industry Regulatory Authority (US)
FSA	Financial Supervisory Authority
FSB	Financial Stability Board
FX	Foreign Currency
ICMA	International Capital Market Association
IG	Investment Grade
IIROC	Investment Industry Regulatory Association of Canada
IM	Investment Memorandum
IOSCO	International Organization of Securities Commissions
IPO	Initial Public Offering
ISIN	International Securities Identification Number
JSDA	Japan Securities Dealers Association
KOIFA	Korea Financial Investment Association
MAR	Market Abuse Regulation
MiFID II	Markets in Financial Instruments Directive II
MiFIR	Markets in Financial Instruments Regulation
MTF	Multilateral Trading Facility
MTN	Medium Term Note
NASD	National Association of Securities Dealers
NCR	Nordic Credit Rating
OECD	Organisation for Economic Co-operation and Development
OTC	Over the Counter
OTF	Organised Trading Facility
SEC	US Securities and Exchange Commission
SI	Systematic Internaliser
SPO	Secondary Public Offering
Takeover Rules	The Swedish Stock Market Self-Regulation Committee's Takeover rules for Nasdaq Stockholm and Nordic Growth Market NGM
TRACE	Trade Reporting and Compliance Engine
Transparency Directive	Directive 2004/109/EC of the European Parliament and of the Council of 15 December 2004 on the harmonisation of transparency requirements in relation to information about issuers whose securities are admitted to trading on a regulated market and amending Directive 2001/34/EC
UK	United Kingdom
US	United States

Executive summary

Since the financial crisis, the Swedish corporate bond market has grown significantly in size and changed in character. The number of issuers has increased manifold and, in parallel, the size of both issues and issuers have decreased substantially. This report provides an extensive mapping of the market, illustrating its transformation over time with respect to market size, issuer characteristics (notably the broadening to include smaller issuers), credit risk, liquidity and market structure. It also includes an international comparison. Drawing from these empirical findings as well as interviews with key institutions and market participants, the report offers a set of policy recommendations (relating to both regulatory and self-regulatory measures) to improve the functioning of the Swedish corporate bond market, with a particular focus on the new issuer profile.

Chapter 1 contains an assessment of the market and the related policy recommendations; Chapter 2 provides a mapping of the Swedish market and its developments; and Chapter 3 compares key aspects of the Swedish market with other markets in the Nordics and the EU, as well as in selected non-EU countries.

Summary of key recommendations

The recommendations are split into seven different areas:

Disclosure at issuance. Under Swedish market practice, a bond offer is typically fully subscribed before a prospectus is published. Investors instead make their decisions based on information contained in a form of investment memorandum, a mostly unregulated and non-standardised document. Market participants have highlighted cases where the investment memorandum omits material information included in the subsequent prospectus, as well as cases of contradictory information between the two documents. In addition, investors have also noted that the time they are given to review the terms of an offer can be unduly short.

Recommendation: Develop self-regulation to ensure that essential information included in the formal prospectus is also included in the investment memorandum. Establish a default review period of circa 10 days, accommodating well-motivated deviations.

Comparability of bond terms. Market participants have indicated that there is significant heterogeneity with respect to the bond terms.

Recommendation: Consider the establishment of a non-normative template of standard bond terms developed by a self-regulatory body, where deviations from the template would need to be disclosed following a comply or explain model.

Equal treatment of bondholders. There is no national regulation that defines the meaning of equal treatment in the context of bondholders. Market participants have indicated that the understanding of what constitutes equal treatment differs among practitioners.

Recommendation: Develop the legal requirement of equal treatment of bondholders. A possible model would be the self-regulatory approach used in the equity markets, where a principle set in law is complemented by self-regulation.

Ongoing disclosure. There is no established understanding of what constitutes inside information for bond issuers according to the EU Market Abuse Regulation (MAR). This may limit transparency and investor protection, especially where issuers only have bonds and no equities listed.

Recommendation: To simplify the application of MAR, consider methods to promote disclosure of inside information by corporate bond issuers.

The role of the agent. As opposed to many other countries, Sweden currently does not have any specific regulation on the role and duties of agents (which act as representatives of bondholders).

Recommendation: Consider the introduction of specific regulation on the role and duties of agents.

Credit ratings. A significant share of Swedish corporate bonds lacks a credit rating. This may limit inflows of institutional investor capital and restrict the ability of regulators and market participants to gauge broader market credit risk.

Recommendation: While positive that investors are not over-dependent on credit ratings, consider if incentives to obtain credit ratings should be increased, in particular for smaller issuers.

Price transparency and secondary market liquidity. Many investors consider price transparency to be inadequate and, as in many other markets, liquidity in the Swedish secondary market is low. This contributes to higher costs of capital for companies through liquidity premia and may exacerbate fire sale pressures during sharp market downturns.

Recommendation: Consider efforts to improve price transparency, benefitting from EU-level developments (notably the MiFIR review). Consider whether issuance of bonds structured in line with the Swedish regulatory authorities' proposed benchmark standard could be encouraged, with due consideration to the possible effects it may have on corporate refinancing risks. In addition, several other recommendations outlined in this report, notably with respect to disclosure and credit ratings, are also expected to contribute to improved liquidity.

Summary of main empirical findings

Significant growth in corporate bond financing. The Swedish corporate bond market for non-financial companies has grown significantly over the past two decades, notably after the 2008 financial crisis. This is partly in response to stricter international banking regulation and efforts to reduce the reliance on bank financing. The average annual amount raised through bonds by Swedish non-financial companies in the period from 2009 to 2023 was more than twice that of the pre-crisis period from 2000 to 2008. By the end of 2023, the total outstanding amount of non-financial corporate bonds was USD 80 billion, almost double the amount at the end of 2008. The share of bond financing in total debt financing has grown faster in Sweden than in peer countries, and is today higher than the euro area average but lower than in the United Kingdom and United States.

Expansion of the market to smaller firms. Until 2008, the Swedish corporate bond market was dominated by a small number of large and established companies within a limited number of industries. However, over the past decade and a half, the share of issuance made up by new issuers has increased significantly, with a simultaneous decrease in the median issue and issuer size. Between 2000 and 2010, the average share of first-time issuers was 23%, which grew to 35% between 2011 and 2023. The median issue size fell from a peak of USD 708 million in 2009 to USD 71 million in 2023. This is a much more significant broadening of the market than can be seen in Nordic peer countries. These developments are indicative of increased accessibility and broader use of corporate bond markets among smaller Swedish companies. This has effectively resulted in a two-tier market, split between very large, internationally active companies, and smaller local companies.

A decrease in credit quality. In parallel to the growth of the market, and in line with global trends, credit quality has continuously decreased in the Swedish market since 2000, and more notably since 2009. This is partly because the non-investment grade segment has grown, from 7% of total outstanding amounts in 2009 to 12% in 2023. However, it is also an effect of decreasing credit quality within the larger investment grade segment. Between 2009 and 2023, the lowest investment grade rating, BBB, represented 53% of average annual investment grade issuance, compared to 11% between 2000 and 2008.

A high share of unrated bonds. The Swedish market has a high share of unrated bonds. Of the total number of issues between 2000 and 2023, 47% did not have a rating from one of the three major international rating agencies or the main local rating agency. This is in line with the other Nordic countries but substantially higher than for example France, the Netherlands and the United States.

Industry concentration and real estate exposure. Real estate companies have gone from representing a negligible share of the Swedish bond market to accounting for as much as 37% of outstanding amounts in 2023, making it the largest industry using the non-financial corporate bond market. A relatively small, but increasing, number of companies represent the majority of bond issuance in the real estate sector. This could potentially lead to market pressures in an environment of tightening monetary conditions and downward price pressure on real estate assets.

A changing ownership landscape. The share of corporate bonds held by domestic pension funds and insurance companies is slightly higher in Sweden than the euro area average, where these investors' shares vary widely from 8% in Germany to 72% in the Netherlands. Direct retail participation in the market is highly limited. Foreign investors are larger owners of Swedish non-financial corporate bonds than domestic ones, holding 63% of total outstanding amounts at the end of the second quarter of 2023. A key recent ownership trend is the growth of investment funds as holders of corporate bonds. At the end of the second quarter of 2023, they represented 37% of domestic ownership, compared to less than 5% in 2008. On the one hand, that has offered increased access to the corporate bond market, in particular for retail investors, and possibly also increased access to market-based debt financing for companies. On the other, it could potentially adversely impact the stability of the market in the absence of proper liquidity management by funds and clear regulatory guidance in this respect.

Limited liquidity and price transparency. Swedish authorities have highlighted low liquidity and limited price transparency as structural issues in the market. The applicable regulations with respect to pre- and post-trade transparency, which are provided in MiFIR/D II, allow for a large number of waivers which has led to a decrease in transparency in the Swedish market. A domestic recommendation has since been implemented to improve transparency, which initial survey results suggest has been helpful. At the EU level, there is political agreement on the review of MiFIR, notably for the establishment of an EU-wide consolidated tape which includes post-trade disclosure of bond transactions. Swedish authorities have proposed the introduction of a benchmark standard for corporate bonds as a possible way to improve liquidity and market functioning. Between 2005-2023, 67% of total issuance by amounts (and 23% by number) fulfilled the proposed benchmark criteria. That figure could have been as high as 90%, using an estimate of bonds that did not conform to the proposed standard but that were issued by companies that could conceivably have issued conforming bonds.

Signs of market pro-cyclicality. Dynamics during the COVID-19 pandemic suggested procyclical tendencies and a lack of resilience under stress in the Swedish corporate bond market, counter to the benefits a well-functioning capital market should be expected to provide. Large segments of the market lost access to financing and several investment funds had to temporarily close due to a lack of reliability in pricing.

1 Assessment and recommendations

This chapter provides an assessment of the Swedish corporate bond market and a set of related recommendations to meet current and future challenges. The recommendations concern both public regulation and self-regulatory bodies. The chapter draws from a detailed mapping of the market and its development over the past two decades (Chapter 2) as well as interviews with key institutions and market participants.

The Swedish corporate bond market has changed significantly over the past twenty years, notably since the 2008 financial crisis. In parallel to rapid growth, there have been changes to both investor borrower profiles, notably with respect to credit risk, industry and size, with an increasing prevalence of smaller issuers.

The regulatory framework for corporate bonds has not developed at pace with the market. To an extent, this is natural: in a dynamic securities market, regulation will respond to market developments with a certain delay, when it can be established that changes are structural and the need for regulation can be clearly identified. However, the structural changes to the Swedish bond market that are documented in this report call for an assessment by regulators and market participants regarding the possible need for new regulation, including self-regulation. This section provides an assessment of the identified issues and the related policy recommendations. The underlying changes that are the basis for the recommendations can primarily be observed among smaller issuers, and to a large extent, the recommendations extend important best practices among larger issuers to the smaller segments of the market. The recommendations focus on Swedish non-financial companies listing bonds.

Addressing these issues, whether through regulatory measures, self-regulatory initiatives (building on the strong tradition of self-regulation in the Swedish market), or a combination thereof, would help improve the functioning of the Swedish corporate bond market. Swedish authorities have highlighted a lack of liquidity and transparency as structural issues in the market. Many of the issues identified in this report relate specifically to transparency, and improvements in these areas would likely contribute to the broader goal of improving liquidity, which is a core aspect of what makes market-based financing a flexible and resilient source of financing.

1.1. Information disclosure at issuance

A prerequisite for an efficient corporate bond market is that the information provided at the time of issuance is complete, consistent and timely. Information asymmetries between issuers and investors should be minimised and the issuer should provide all available information relevant to bond pricing to market participants on equal terms. The rapid growth of the Swedish corporate bond market and the entrance of many smaller issuers have limited the extent to which these requirements are satisfied.

As a general rule, the EU Prospectus Regulation requires and prescribes the content of a detailed offering document to be prepared in connection with a corporate bond issue. However, due to Swedish and broader EU market practice, issues are generally exempt from this requirement since the unit value of a bond is set to at least EUR 100 000 and the issue is directed only to qualified investors. Instead, the offer information to investors is typically provided in the form of an investment memorandum. This offer practice is used in the majority of non-financial corporate bond offers in Sweden today. However, there is no specific regulation or standard to guide neither the content, nor the review period of the investment memoranda.

Moreover, there are no specific regulations related to liability with respect to the accuracy of the information provided by an issuer that is using an investment memorandum or equivalent document other than a prospectus. This means that an investor in a corporate bond issue who has suffered damages due to deficiencies or inaccuracies in the issue documentation, such as the investment memorandum, must rely on general tort law rules on misleading marketing, which is likely to involve significant uncertainties and costs. More generally, the Swedish Financial Services Authority's (FSA) analysis of prospectus liability has found that many actors consider that there are few or no possibilities to claim liability from legal persons for information in a prospectus, or that the legal situation is difficult to assess, even in cases where the rules on prospectus liability are applicable (Finansinspektionen, 2021[1]).

If a company wants to broaden its investor base by listing the bond for public trading, a listing prospectus needs to be prepared in accordance with the Prospectus Regulation, even if the issue itself was done with an investment memorandum. Market participants have noted that best practice is that the essential information provided in the listing prospectus should also have been included in the initial investment memorandum. Nevertheless, interviews suggest that it is not uncommon for the investment memorandum to lack essential company-specific information that is subsequently included in the listing prospectus. Examples where the two documents contain contradictory information have also been highlighted. **Against this background, it is recommended that self-regulation be developed to ensure that essential information included in the formal prospectus, whenever possible, is also included in the initial investment memorandum.** In addition, given the practice of using investment memoranda as the basis for investment, having company management (such as the CEO or the CFO) signing off to verify the accuracy of the information provided in these documents and its compliance with Article 22.3–4 of the Prospectus Regulation as a standard practice could help improve market trust.

Contractual freedom and variability with respect to the terms of a bond issue is part of a sound market process of finding financial solutions that suit both issuers and investors. In order for the bond market to benefit from this process, it is necessary that also qualified investors are given sufficient time to properly evaluate the sometimes complex and idiosyncratic contractual terms of a bond offer. However, several investors have testified that the time they are given to review and assess the terms of an offer can be unduly short. This may discourage participation as well as limit the possibilities of applying tailored and idiosyncratic terms that after proper analysis may prove to be an efficient financial solution for both the company and the investor. **In order to mitigate these risks, it is recommended that market participants establish a default review period of circa 10 days.**

The introduction of such a default standard for reviewing investment memoranda would, for example, be in line with the required acceptance period that apply under the Swedish Securities Market Self-Regulation Committee's Takeover Rules (2021[2]) for both regulated markets and certain trading platforms. However, the introduction of a default review period should account for the fact that the issuer in some cases may be under considerable time pressure to obtain financing. In other cases, such as investment grade tap-issues or issuance under an established medium-term note (MTN) programme, investors are generally unlikely to need a particularly long review period. **Any self-regulatory provisions with respect to review periods should accommodate well motivated deviations from the default review period.**

1.2. Comparability of bond terms

Disclosure should not only be complete, consistent and timely. A well-functioning market also requires that information is comparable across different bond issues. This may become a challenge when the number of issues increases and there is large variation in the design, definition, and use of bond covenants. Market participants, in particular investors, have therefore indicated an interest in ways to improve comparability of bond terms.

The starting point for the design and use of bond terms is the freedom of contract, which is assumed to bring efficient financing solutions for both investors and companies. Any deviations from this principle must therefore be well motivated. The tradition in Swedish civil law is to limit this freedom of contract only when the relationships between the parties in a contractual situation are unequal (e.g. consumer protection) or in the event of market failures.

In order to improve comparability of bond terms while safeguarding the freedom of contract, it is recommended that a self-regulatory body establishes a template for the standard non-commercial terms used in Swedish corporate bond issues intended for the Swedish market, considering the differences between standalone issues and issues within programmes. The template could for instance cover the terms regarding the bondholder meeting and important decisions such as change of terms and majority provisions, the role of the agent and disclosure.

Such a template could be based on the main principles of the Swedish Securities Markets Association's standard terms and conditions for bonds and be applied on a "comply or explain" basis. The template would then serve as the default standard for how bond terms should be presented and explained regarding certain areas. A company issuing under the standard bond terms would simply state that its offer is in line with the standard template (in the areas covered by the template). If the bond terms or terminology deviate from the agreed template, this would be added in a brief note explaining why these differences occur and what they imply. This approach could also be applied to specific market segments (e.g. non-investment grade and unrated bonds), as deemed necessary by market participants.

A complementary means to achieve comparability is through increased standardisation. One way to do this is to further encourage a voluntary Swedish benchmark standard as suggested by the Swedish FSA, the National Debt Office and the Riksbank (see section 2.8.2).

1.3. Equal treatment of bondholders

Equal treatment of investors is one of the core tenets of Swedish capital market regulation. The Swedish Securities Market Act (Chapter 18, Section 3) provides a requirement of equal treatment of bondholders with regard to information, which implements Article 18(1) of the EU Transparency Directive (Lidman, 2023[3]). Contrary to what applies on the stock market, however, there is currently no general rule on equal treatment of bondholders in Swedish law, and there is no national case law or other source of law that provides other specific rules on equal treatment. Market participants have indicated that the understanding of the requirement differs among practitioners, resulting in cases where bondholders are not treated equally, including with regard to access to information, bond buybacks, early redemptions and award of consent fees.

Developing a common understanding of equal treatment on the bond market is particularly relevant in the context of extensive growth which has resulted in a certain degree of heterogeneity in the market. The self-regulatory approach of the Swedish equity market may serve as a reference point; core principles of equal or equivalent treatment in, for instance, the Swedish Companies Act are complemented by self-regulatory rules on private placements, rules on equal treatment of target company shareholders in takeover bids[1] and statements by the Swedish Securities Council.[2]

Given the effectiveness and strong tradition of self-regulation in Sweden, such a model, in which market participants develop rules on equal treatment through self-regulation, should also be feasible for the corporate bond market. Examples of areas where the meaning of equal treatment could be clarified include information exchanges between the issuer (or agent) and the bondholders; repurchases and early redemptions; and events of changes to the terms and conditions (for example in award of a consent fee).

It is recommended that a general requirement of equal treatment of bondholders is introduced in law, and that it is supplemented by market participants through self-regulation that develop its application and meaning. Such an approach can be modelled on the Swedish Takeover Rules and other equity market regulation, where self-regulation and numerous rulings by the Swedish Securities Council have established a clear understanding of the principle of equal treatment.

1.4. Ongoing disclosure of price-sensitive information

An issuer whose securities are admitted to trading on a regulated market or a multilateral trading facility (MTF) is required to disclose inside information under Articles 7 and 17 of the EU Market Abuse Regulation (MAR) (European Parliament and the Council of the European Union, 2014[4]). This disclosure obligation is complex and virtually all case law and literature in this area is focused on the disclosure of inside information with regard to issuers of equity. Given the generally higher sensitivity of the price of a share compared to the price of a bond, information other than that which relates directly to the bonds themselves as securities will rarely be considered inside information exclusively in relation to bonds, but will also be considered inside information with respect to shares. In these cases, it is therefore relatively easy to obtain guidance on what constitutes inside information in a company and how to treat it. However, for companies that only have bonds admitted to trading there is effectively no guidance, and the disclosure requirements for these companies are not deemed clear.

To promote disclosure and the application of MAR, it is therefore recommended to explore methods involving market participants to increase the disclosure of inside information by corporate bond issuers.

Examples of issues in need of clarification include:

1. The types of information that in principle always constitute inside information (e.g. significant risk of default, planned changes to bond terms, planned repurchases, significant risk of credit rating downgrades)
2. How disclosure should be managed when there is a risk of default
3. If and when favourable information about the company's performance may constitute inside information
4. Whether the assessment of what constitutes inside information may differ according to the type of issuer (e.g. investment grade versus non-investment grade issuers).

1.5. The role of the agent

For most Swedish non-investment grade bonds, an agent[3] is appointed with the authority to represent bondholders in relation to the issuer and to safeguard their interests as an investor group. The agent is formally appointed by the issuer, and in practice on the recommendation of the arranging bank (alternatively, as is often the case for investment grade bonds, the duties of the agent are carried out directly by the arranging bank).

Contrary to other Nordic countries, there is no specific Swedish regulation on the role and duties of the agent beyond general rules on representatives and proxies. This has raised several calls for relevant regulation, including from Swedish industry (Confederation of Swedish Enterprise, 2012[5]).

There is specific legislation on the role and duty of the agent in Denmark and Finland. In Norway, where agents have been present in the market since 1993 when *Norsk tillitsmann ASA* was founded,[4] agents are regulated by case law and through market practice.[5] The Finnish as well as the Danish law is detailed and deals with, among other things, the selection of agent, the legal effect of the agency agreement, the requirement that the agent must treat bondholders equally, its right to represent the bondholders in various ways, and other duties towards the bondholders.[6]

To address possible conflicts of interest and to ensure the right of legal representation, it is recommended that specific rules concerning the role of the agent be introduced in Swedish law, in line with other Nordic countries.

1.6. Credit ratings among smaller issuers

Forty-eight percent of all Swedish issues between 2000 and 2023 did not have a rating from one of the three main international rating agencies. While other Nordic countries are also characterised by a high portion of unrated bonds, it is well above some other European markets and the United States (see Figure 3.6).

To a large extent, this can be explained by the relatively small size of certain Swedish issuers and their bonds (see Figure 2.11). Small issue sizes can make obtaining a rating from the major international credit rating agencies (S&P, Moody's and Fitch) prohibitively expensive. S&P data show that the cost of a credit rating generally amounts to 0.071% of the total transaction value, with a minimum cost of USD 110 000, which in practice means that all issues below USD 155 million will entail a cost of more than 0.071%. There are also additional annual costs associated with having a credit rating. This means that for a bond issue of USD 71 million, which was the median size in Sweden in 2023, the total cost would be 0.15%. Another factor that may discourage ratings among smaller companies is the positive correlation between the size of the company and the credit rating (OECD, 2021[6]). A third possible contributing factor relates to market practice. Until 2018, several major Swedish banks issued so-called shadow ratings, where they assigned credit ratings to issuers on a scale similar to that used by the main international rating agencies. However, these activities ceased following rulings by ESMA in 2018 concluding that they were in breach of the Credit Rating Agencies Regulation (ESMA, 2018[7]). Thus far, the disappearance of shadow ratings has not been offset by an increased use of "official" ratings among non-financial companies. In 2016, rating company Nordic Credit Rating was set up by large banks and institutions in the region to lower the threshold for small and mid-sized issuers to obtain a credit rating.

Because of their significance to institutional investors and indexing strategies, credit ratings can play an important role in bond market development. Widespread use of credit ratings also gives both regulators and investors a broad measure to gauge credit risk in a market. The relatively high share of unrated bonds in Sweden could therefore be a detriment to further market development.

It is recommended to consider means and incentives to increase the use of credit ratings by smaller issuers.

Means and incentives to increase the use of credit ratings (local or international) naturally need to take the typical issuer profile and size of the market into account – introducing a simple credit rating requirement for bond issuers (or a category thereof) would likely not be appropriate, given the significance of the associated cost to smaller issuers. Some countries, recognising the disincentives for smaller issuers to obtain credit ratings, have introduced systems where credit ratings are provided nationally at a lower cost. In France, for example, the *Banque de France* provides a form of credit rating for individual companies for a fee through the FIBEN system. Another possible measure, aligned with local practices, could be the "comply or explain" model discussed in section 1.2, whereby issuers would be obliged to either obtain a credit rating or explain why they have chosen not to.

1.7. Price transparency and secondary market liquidity

Section 2.8 highlights the decrease in price transparency on the Swedish market following the implementation of MiFID II and MiFIR in 2018. Surveys of market participants suggest that a lack of transparency in pricing and trading has led to unreliable pricing. In response to these developments, in 2020 the Swedish FSA commissioned the Swedish Securities Markets Association (SSMA) to examine ways to improve transparency. This resulted in a recommendation on voluntary transparency rules in addition to the mandatory MiFIR/D II rules, which appears to have been generally well-received. However, many investors still consider price transparency to be inadequate.

In addition, an EU-level review of MiFIR is currently underway, partly with the aim of improving price transparency in the markets. The European Commission presented its proposal for an amending directive at the beginning of 2021. The European Parliament presented its preliminary position on the proposal in July 2022, and a political agreement was reached in June 2023, including the creation of a mandatory framework for a consolidated tape, which is set to include post-trade bond data (European Commission, 2023[8]).

A related issue has to do with secondary market liquidity. A large empirical literature documents the connection between transparency and bond market liquidity/transaction costs, often suggesting increased transparency has beneficial effects on these areas (see e.g. (Edwards, Lawrence and Piwowar, 2007[9]; Goldstein, Hotchkiss and Sirri, 2007[10]; Bessembinder and Maxwell, 2008[11]; Brugler, Comerton-Forde and Martin, 2022[12])). The lack of liquidity in Sweden has been highlighted as a policy concern by the Swedish Riksbank, the Swedish National Debt Office and the Swedish FSA (see e.g. (Wollert, 2020[13]) as well as Finansinspektionen (2021[14]) and (2022[15])). An objection that is sometimes made against increased price transparency is that it may reduce incentives for dealer activity, thus reducing liquidity. This debate was prominent during the introduction of the Trade Reporting and Compliance Engine (TRACE) system in the United States in the early 2000s, and the reason why it was phased in gradually. However, dealer activity has remained rather high and no significant detrimental effects on dealer-provided liquidity have been observed following the introduction of TRACE (see further section 2.7).

Low corporate bond market liquidity is not unique to the Swedish market. As further discussed in section 2.8, this partly has to do with the nature of the instrument: fixed income securities like corporate bonds pay defined amounts over their lifetime and are redeemed at a set time, making them well-suited for long-term buy-and-hold investors that need predictable cash flows to match their liabilities. The nature of a debt contract also means that the market value of a bond does not have upside exposure to positive developments in the issuer's business in the way that shares do, meaning the incentives for trading are not the same as for equities. Lower levels of liquidity than in equity markets are therefore natural and should be expected. However, it is important to promote liquidity to the extent possible, as excessively low liquidity in the secondary market is associated with higher costs of capital and spreads in the primary market (see e.g. (Longstaff, Mithal and Neis, 2005[16]; Chen, Lesmond and Wei, 2007[17]; Bao, Pan and Wang, 2011[18])). In addition, low liquidity can exacerbate the negative effects of fire sale pressures in times of crisis, as was arguably the case in Sweden during the pandemic-induced crisis in 2020 (see section 2.8.1).

Liquidity is typically defined as a measure of market participants' ability to carry out transactions without triggering price changes. A liquid bond market can thus be said to be a market that enables the purchase and sale of large quantities of securities at any time and at low transaction costs. In addition to adequate levels of transparency, this requires a large, broad and heterogeneous investor base (Li and Yu, 2022[19]). Regulation plays a role in promoting both of these things, and several of the proposed measures outlined in this report would contribute to increased liquidity: increased disclosure in connection with issues; increased comparability of bond terms; better regular disclosure; and increased use of credit ratings would all serve to increase investor confidence and lower the cost of information collection. Clearer requirements for equal treatment and regulation of the role of the agent would likely further strengthen investor protection and lead to possible reductions in the cost of information collection, bargaining and monitoring.

As discussed under section 2.8.2, one proposal to improve liquidity, put forward jointly by the Swedish Riksbank, the FSA and the National Debt Office, is to create a benchmark standard for Swedish corporate bonds. One reason companies may be hesitant to issue benchmark bonds relates to refinancing risk. By having a larger share of outstanding debt tied up in one instrument, an issuer is more exposed to low market demand and/or tighter financial conditions when the debt needs to be refinanced. Companies may therefore have incentives to issue several smaller bonds to spread out repayment, decreasing this risk. On the other hand, the regulatory rationale for increasing the use of benchmark bonds is to increase liquidity, which would serve to decrease refinancing risks. To overcome this coordination problem, where optimal decisions at the firm-level could arguably lead to sub-optimal outcomes at the market level, it could be explored whether regulatory/fiscal incentives would help shift issuers towards benchmark issues. Section 2.8.2 provides an estimate of existing and assessed potential benchmark issues in the Swedish market.

Price transparency should be improved. Together with other measures to improve market functioning outlined in this report, this would likely contribute to improved secondary market liquidity. Domestic policy measures should also make sure to benefit from the development of an

EU-level consolidated tape. Given experiences in other markets, including the United States following the introduction of TRACE, the potential negative effects on dealer activity of increased price transparency should be monitored but may not be a major concern.

2 Mapping the Swedish corporate bond market landscape

This chapter provides an overview of how the Swedish non-financial corporate bond market has developed over the past two decades with respect to size, risk profile and issuer characteristics. It also examines the investor base and provides a description of secondary market activity. The chapter includes a case study of the COVID-19 pandemic's effect on the Swedish non-financial corporate bond market, as well as an overview of the real estate sector's increasing use of corporate bond markets.

2.1. Introduction and universe of analysis

This chapter provides an overview of developments in the Swedish corporate bond market. The analysis is limited to bond-issuing companies headquartered in Sweden that are active in the non-financial sector. Companies operating in the real estate sector are not considered part of the non-financial universe (sections 2.2 to 2.8) but are analysed separately in section 2.9. No restrictions are applied with respect to currency or market of issuance unless specifically stated.

2.2. Market size

The Swedish corporate bond market for non-financial companies is relatively young and has changed significantly over the past two decades. Between 2000 and 2008, growth was muted and the market was largely characterised by a small number of large companies within a limited number of industries. However, in the years following the 2008 financial crisis, notably as access to bank lending diminished, the market began expanding. In real terms, issuance by non-financial companies averaged USD 6.7 billion annually between 2000 and 2008. This more than doubled to USD 13.8 billion in the period between 2009 and 2023 (Figure 2.1, Panel A).

As a comparison, the average total annual amounts of equity (primary and secondary offerings) issued by non-financial companies during these periods were USD 7.4 billion and USD 9.4 billion, respectively. In other words, bond issuance surpassed equity issuance. This is notable given the prevalence of equity financing in Sweden, which has one of the most active equity markets in the EU, both with respect to size and the number of listed companies (Eurofi, 2023[20]). However, the size difference between corporate bond and equity markets remains much smaller in Sweden than in larger markets. For example, since 2009, average annual bond issuance in Sweden has been 1.5 times larger than total average annual equity issuance, compared to 5.9 times in the United States and 3.7 in the EU. The fact that bond issuance has overtaken equity issuance in size is nevertheless an illustration of the pace at which the Swedish market is growing. At the end of 2023, the total amount of outstanding non-financial corporate bonds was USD 80 billion, almost twice the amount in 2008 (Figure 2.1, Panel B).

Figure 2.1. The size of the Swedish non-financial corporate bond market

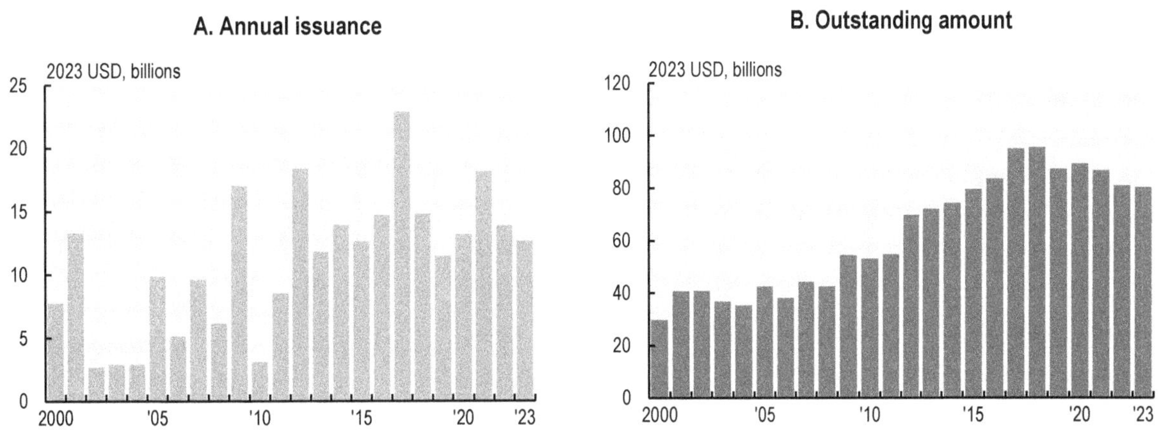

Source: OECD Capital Market Series dataset, LSEG, see Annex for details.

As a consequence, debt securities, notably corporate bonds, have increased as a share of total corporate debt financing, meaning that market-based debt financing has grown faster than bank loans. Having remained remarkably stable between 9% and 11% from 2000 to 2012, the share of debt securities in total debt financing had grown to 16% in the second quarter of 2023, the vast majority of which is made up by long-term securities (Figure 2.2, Panel A). The share of debt securities in total debt financing is slightly higher than in the euro area, but lower than in other regions where market-based financing is more developed (see further discussion under Chapter 3). Sweden remains a largely bank-dependent economy, with loans representing 84% of non-financial companies' aggregate debt financing (Figure 2.2, Panel B).

Figure 2.2. Swedish non-financial companies' use of debt securities and bank loans

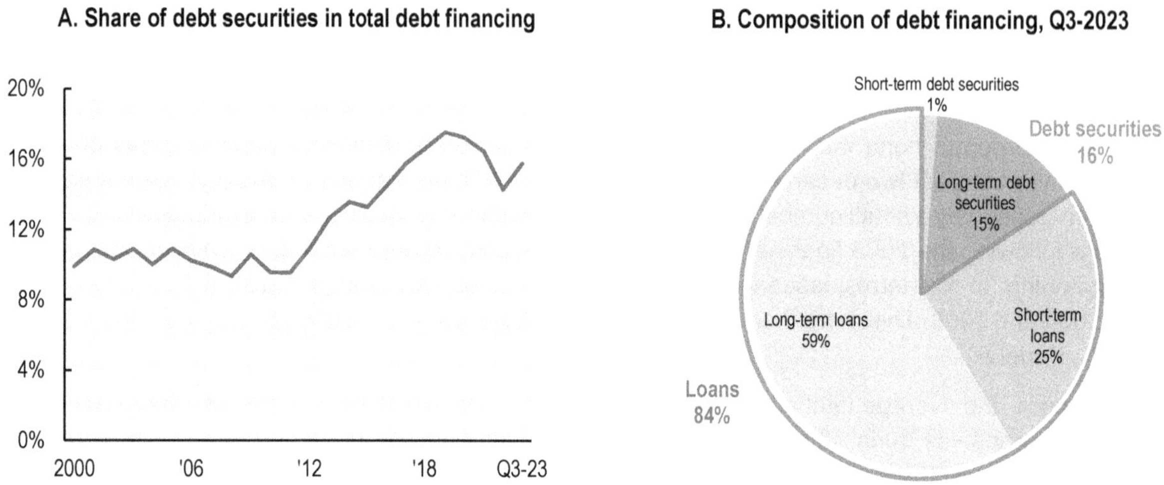

Note: Panel A shows the share of debt securities (long and short-term) in total debt financing (the sum of total loans and total debt securities) for non-financial companies. Securities with original maturities below one year are classified as short-term.
Source: ECB.

2.3. Credit risk profile

Looking at the risk profile of the Swedish corporate bond market reveals several notable trends. Firstly, as seen in Panel A of Figure 2.3, the credit quality of Swedish bond issuances has followed the global decreasing trend in credit quality starting, in 2000 and more notably since 2009 when market growth accelerated. For bonds issued in 2023, the average value-weighted rating was just below BBB+. This is an increase of a full notch since 2021, when the average rating was just above BBB-, the lowest investment grade rating. This increase reflects more restrictive financial conditions following the increase in interest rates during 2022 and 2023.

To some extent, the longer-term decrease in credit quality is driven by investors accepting higher risk in search for higher yields in the general low-yield environment that prevailed following the extensive expansionary monetary policies implemented by several central banks around the world in the wake of the 2008 financial crisis, and more recently in response to the euro and COVID-19 crises. Notably, the Swedish Riksbank was the first central bank to bring its main repurchase rate into negative territory in early 2015.

Another notable development is the prevalence of BBB rated bonds in the composition of investment grade issuance. In 2023, BBB rated bonds accounted for 54% of total issuance, up from an average of less than 11% over the period 2000-08. In 2021, BBB issuance represented 76% of total rated issuance (Figure 2.3, Panel B). Over time, by far the largest corresponding decrease has taken place in the A grade category. This increase in the weight of the lowest credit quality category within investment grade issuance is also in line with global trends.

Figure 2.3. Credit ratings of Swedish non-financial bonds

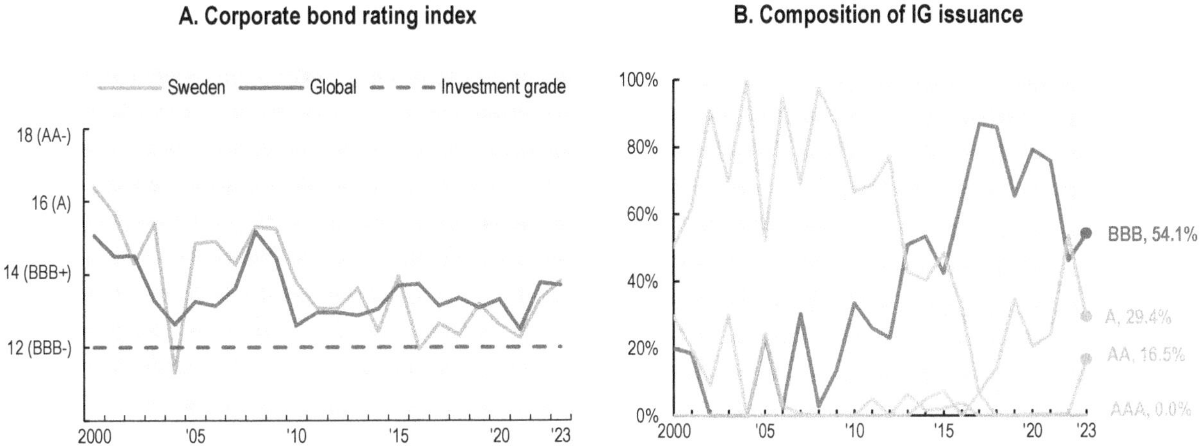

Note: Refers to ratings by S&P, Moody's and Fitch. The index shown in Panel A is constructed by assigning a score of 1 to a bond if it has the lowest credit rating and 21 if it has the highest rating. The corporate bond rating index is then calculated by averaging individual bond scores, weighted by issue amounts.
Source: OECD Capital Market Series dataset, LSEG, see Annex for details.

A significant portion of Swedish bonds are unrated. Of the total number of issues between 2000 and 2023, 48% did not have a rating by one of the three major international rating agencies. Including ratings from the local credit rating agency, Nordic Credit Rating, only makes a marginal difference, bringing the unrated share down to 47%. Of the rated bonds, 87% were investment grade (Figure 2.4, Panel A). It is worth noting that when looking at amounts rather than number of bonds, the share of unrated bonds is significantly lower at 21%. This is to be expected, since larger issuances typically target a broader, often international investor base that require the bonds they invest in to have credit ratings from the major agencies. As shown in Panel B of Figure 2.4, the share of unrated bonds has increased rather significantly over time, notably since 2010. This is in line with the expansion of the market to smaller companies that are less likely to obtain a credit rating (see Figure 2.11 and related discussion). In 2023, the median issuer with a credit rating in Sweden was well above twice as big as the median unrated issuer.

According to the Swedish Riksbank (2014[21]), in 2014 about two-thirds of the unrated bonds issued in Sweden were categorised as investment grade by domestic banks in their internal ratings. However, this practice of domestic banks supplying so-called "shadow ratings" has since been discontinued, after the European Securities and Markets Authority (ESMA) found it to be in breach of the Credit Rating Agencies Regulation (CRAR) and consequently fined five major Nordic banks (ESMA, 2018[7]).

Having a credit rating from one of the main international rating agencies is often a prerequisite for accessing capital from many types of institutional investors, especially foreign, who use credit ratings as an aggregate risk management tool for large portfolios and do not necessarily have business models that allow for detailed due diligence of individual bonds. Certain institutional investors, notably pension funds and insurance companies, are also constrained by regulation to holdings above a certain rating.

One reason for the high proportion of unrated bonds in Sweden is likely the fact that obtaining a rating from the major international rating agencies involves significant costs that may be prohibitive for smaller issuers. For example, S&P Global Ratings has disclosed that credit ratings for most transactions involve a fee of up to 7.1 basis points of the total transaction value, with a floor of USD 110 000, meaning that any issue below USD 155 million will carry a cost above 7.1 basis points.[7] For a bond issue of USD 71 million – the median size in Sweden in 2023 – the cost would be 15.5 basis points. In addition, all else equal, a larger company size is associated with a higher rating, possibly further discouraging smaller issuers from obtaining ratings. Scale (e.g. total sales) is one of the five factors Moody's uses to assign its ratings (OECD, 2021[6]).

In 2016, rating company Nordic Credit Rating was set up by large banks and institutions in the region to lower the threshold for small and mid-sized issuers to obtain a credit rating. Recognising the existence of the dynamics favouring larger issuers as well as the need for an active market for research on creditworthiness of smaller companies, some countries have implemented systems where ratings are provided nationally at reduced cost. This is done with the understanding that smaller size issues are typically not intended for large, international investors who would require a rating from (at least) one of the established agencies, but that it is beneficial to have easily accessible information that can help investors gauge default risks. For example, in France the *Banque de France* provides a form of credit score for individual firms for a fee through the FIBEN system (OECD, 2020[22]). In Norway, self-regulation has recently been introduced to incentivise the use of ratings by so called "bond funds" (VVF, 2023[23]).

Figure 2.4. Rated and unrated issues, Swedish non-financial corporate bonds

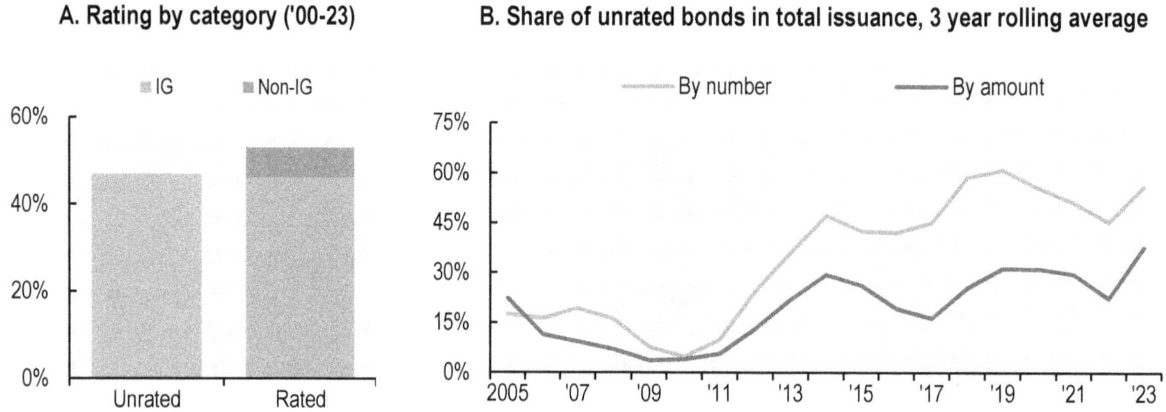

Note: Includes ratings from S&P, Moody's, Fitch as well as local agency Nordic Credit Rating. Panel A shows shares by number of bonds.
Source: OECD Capital Market Series dataset, LSEG, Nordic Credit Rating, see Annex for details.

At the end of 2023, the non-investment grade segment of the Swedish non-financial bond market made up 12.4% of total outstanding amounts, including unrated bonds. This is roughly in line with the share of outstanding non-investment grade bonds globally, which is 13.6%. The Swedish share has increased somewhat as the market has grown. The lowest share was recorded in 2010 at 5.3%, after three years without non-investment grade issuance in 2006, 2008 and 2009. It peaked at 16.5% in 2017 (Figure 2.5, Panel A).

While the outstanding share of non-investment grade bonds has increased since 2010, this only partially explains the downward trend in the rating index shown in Panel A of Figure 2.3. This indicates that the main driver of lower ratings is a change in the composition of investment grade issuance, as shown in Panel B of Figure 2.3. Notably, the value-weighted average rating in the non-investment grade category has not been declining (Figure 2.5, Panel B). If anything, it has shown a slight upward trend, although with relatively significant swings over time.

Figure 2.5. The Swedish non-investment grade corporate bond market

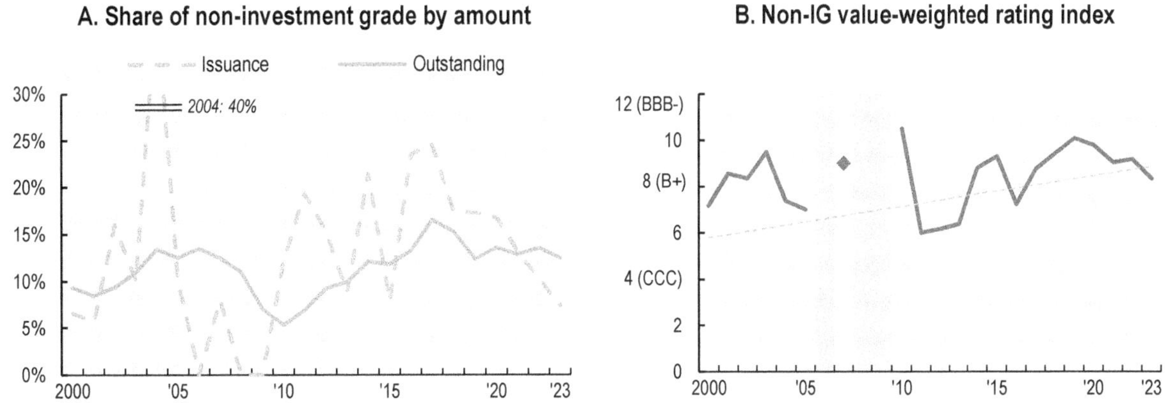

Note: Shaded areas in Panel B represent years with no non-investment grade issuance. The index shown in Panel B is constructed by assigning a score of 1 to a bond if it has the lowest credit rating and 21 if it has the highest rating. The corporate bond rating index is then calculated by averaging individual bond scores for non-investment grade issuers (< 12), weighted by issue amounts.
Source: OECD Capital Market Series dataset, LSEG, see Annex for details.

An important aspect of the risk level of a bond market is the aggregate maturity and repayment profile. Equal-weighted average maturity at issuance has been decreasing over time. Between 2000-07 the average maturity was 6.6 years, compared to 6.0 years between 2008-23 and 4.8 years in 2023. The median maturity is slightly lower at 4.2 years at the end of 2023, and lower still when considering only bonds denominated in the domestic currency, for which it was 4.0 years.

Since 2008, Swedish investment grade bond maturities have on average been 2 years longer than those of non-investment grade bonds, a difference which is smaller than the global one during the same period (4.1 years). Since the ratio between the average maturity of investment grade and non-investment grade bonds in Sweden is similar to the global ratio, it follows that the divergence is driven by generally shorter average maturities in Sweden.

When companies have large amounts of debt coming due within a short time period, they may be exposed to refinancing risk, especially when financial conditions are significantly tighter than when the existing debt stock was issued. If a large share of total outstanding bonds is coming due under such conditions, it may amplify existing shocks with detrimental effects on the real economy. Panel B of Figure 2.6 illustrates the bond debt coming due within the next three years and its share of the total outstanding bond debt. The amount due in the next three years has increased substantially since the 2008 financial crisis, almost quadrupling since 2009. It has also increased as a share of total outstanding bonds, although the increase is less pronounced than for absolute amounts. In 2023, it stood at 51%. It is worth noting that the share was at its lowest in 2009 (at 20%), when crisis-induced risk aversion likely drove investors towards safer issuers who were able to issue at longer maturities. The Swedish non-investment grade market was effectively frozen in both 2008 and 2009, with zero issuance in both years.

Figure 2.6. Maturity and repayment profile of Swedish non-financial bonds

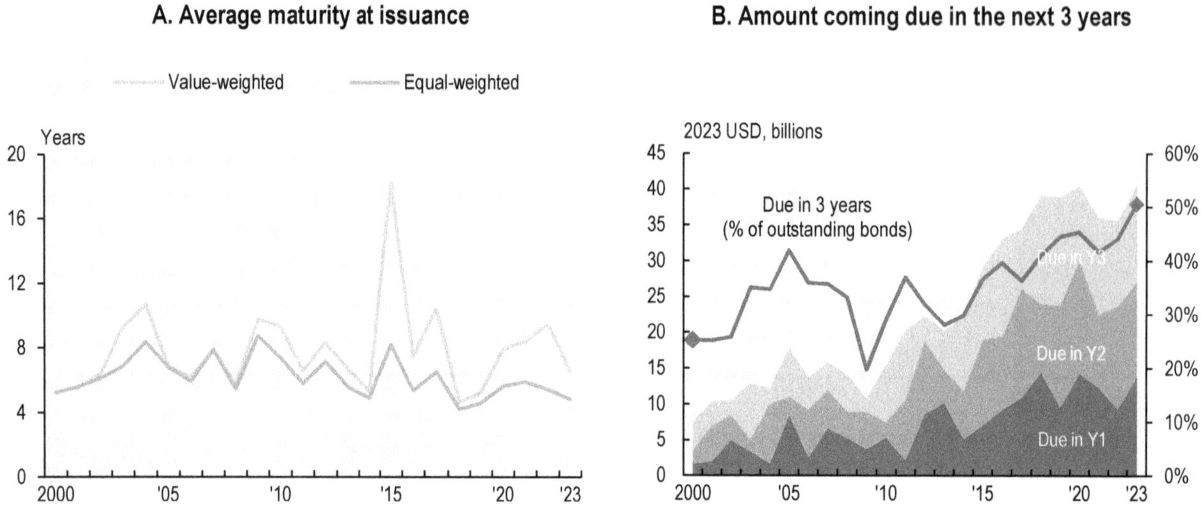

Note: The peak in 2015 in Panel A is driven by a set of four large bonds (between USD 344 million to USD 1.05 billion) issued by state-owned power company Vattenfall with maturities between 62 and 63 years.
Source: OECD Capital Market Series dataset, LSEG, see Annex for details.

Between 2000 and 2023, bonds denominated in euros made up 56% of total Swedish non-financial issuance, followed by the Swedish Krona (SEK) at 33%. Most of the remainder was issued in US dollars (Figure 2.7, Panel A). Until 2010, issuance in SEK was minimal (with the exception of 2007 and 2008) and the market was dominated by euro denominated bonds.[8] However, as the market expanded and became accessible to a larger number of companies around 2010, the share of domestic currency bonds increased sharply. Between 2010 and 2023, the share of SEK-denominated bonds in total issuance averaged 45%, compared to 8% in the period from 2000 to 2011. In 2023, the share was 53% (Panel B). Panel C shows the average and median size of bonds issued in the two different currencies, clearly illustrating how bonds (and issuers) issued to the international markets (proxied by euro denomination) and the domestic ones (in SEK) differ in character. The average (median) size of Swedish corporate bonds issued in euros between 2000 and 2023 was USD 539 (481) million, more than five times the amount in SEK, which was USD 98 (70) million. With this in mind, the increasing share of SEK issuance shown in Panel B is another indicator of the growing access of smaller, domestic companies to the Swedish bond market.

Figure 2.7. Currency composition of Swedish non-financial bond issuance

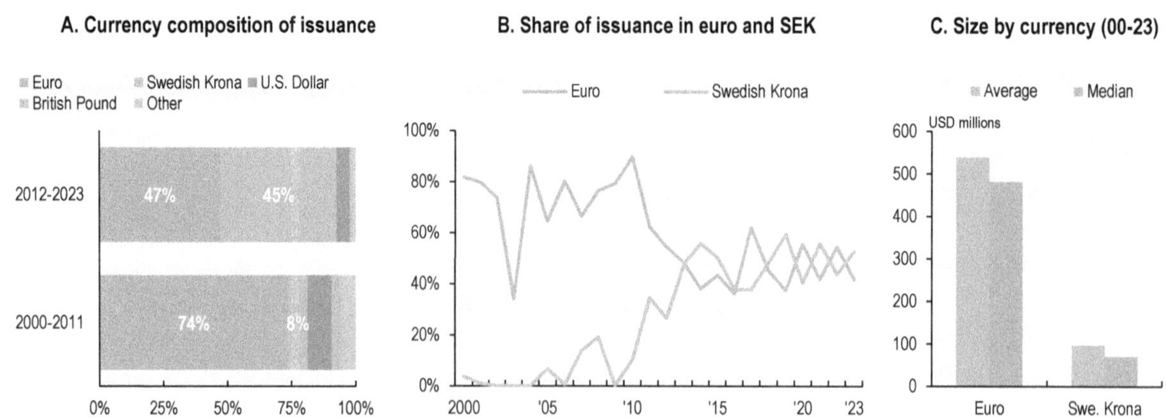

Note: Panels A and B both show shares of the total amount issued.
Source: OECD Capital Market Series dataset, LSEG, see Annex for details.

Data on the exchanges used for listings are consistent with this development. Whereas international exchanges are dominant when looking at total issuance amounts between 2000 to 2023, local exchanges is the largest category when looking at number of issues. Specifically, Luxembourg is the most important foreign exchange, with 40% of the listed amount during the last two decades, followed by London at 18%, equal to the share of Swedish exchanges. A relatively sizeable share of bonds is classified as unlisted (10%) and over-the-counter (5%). Non-investment grade bonds are more commonly unlisted than investment grade ones (18% versus 7% by amount from 2000 to 2023). Looking at the number of issues, 41% are listed on domestic exchanges (Figure 2.8, Panel A).

Also in line with the growing prevalence of domestic currency denominated bonds shown above, Panel B of Figure 2.8 shows how the share of local exchange issuance has increased over time. Similar to the development in SEK-denominated issuance, the share of locally listed bonds was effectively zero up until 2011, after which it has grown substantially, peaking at 44% in 2021. It bears mentioning that while most Swedish corporate bonds are listed on an exchange, trading is effectively exclusively done OTC (see section 2.8).

Figure 2.8. Issuance by exchange

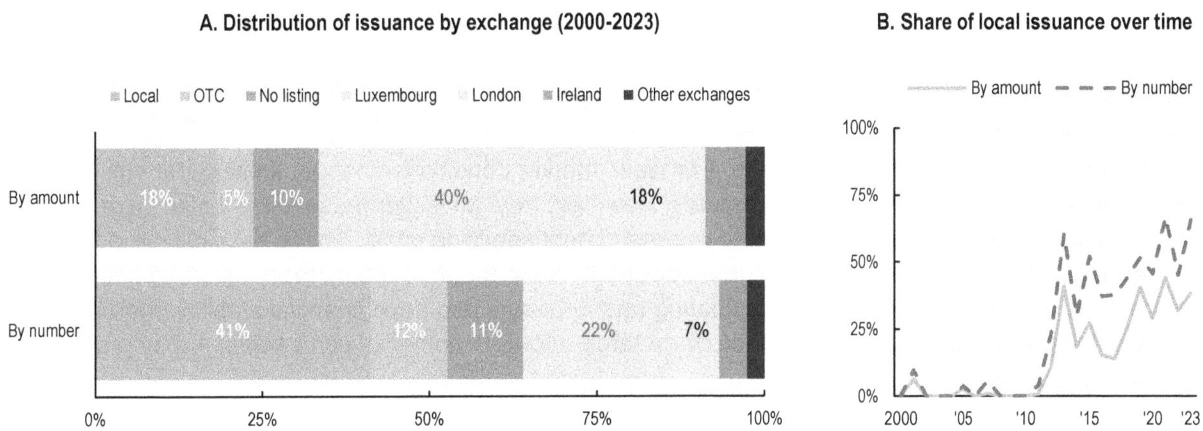

Note: The following exchanges are included in the Local category: Stockholm/Nasdaq Nordic and NGM Nordic MTF.
Source: OECD Capital Market Series dataset, LSEG, see Annex for details.

Looking at exchanges and currency denomination in conjunction shows more clearly the types of bonds that are issued in different markets. Figure 2.9 shows the significant difference in currency composition by exchange. On local exchanges, 87% of all bonds issued (by amount) between 2000 and 2023 were denominated in SEK, with euro-denominated issues making up the clear majority of the remaining 11%. The domestic currency share is also substantial for bonds classified as OTC, at 83%. Contrarily, on foreign exchanges euro-denominated bonds represent as much as 77% of issuance and the Swedish krona 15%. For bonds without listings the US dollar is the single largest currency, representing 43% of issuance.[9]

Figure 2.9. Currency distribution of issuance by exchange, 2000-23

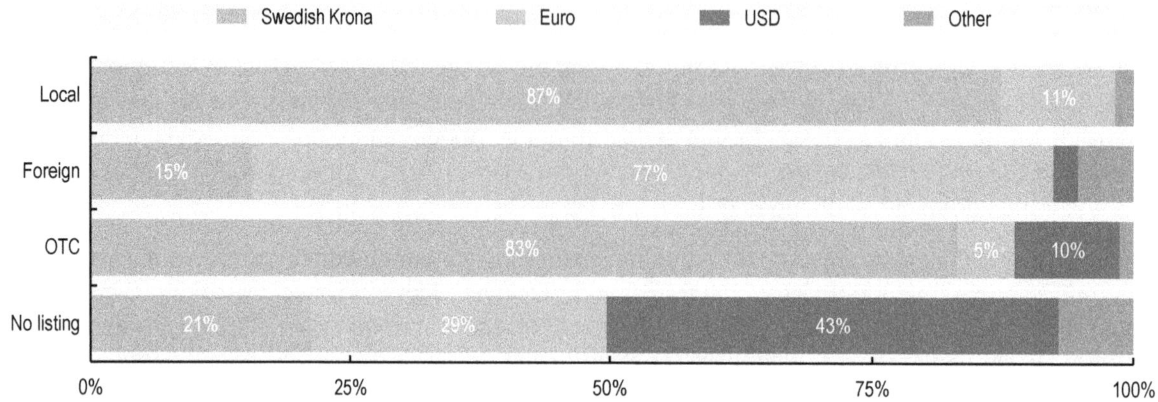

Note: The following exchanges are included in the Local category: Stockholm/Nasdaq Nordic and NGM Nordic MTF.
Source: OECD Capital Market Series dataset, LSEG, see Annex for details.

Turning to interest rate structures, the share of floating-rate bonds in total amounts issued in Sweden has increased significantly in the past decade, from 18% in 2010 to 38% in 2023 (Figure 2.10). This is substantially higher than in other advanced economies, where the aggregate share of floating rate issuance for non-financial companies since 2008 has only been 6% (OECD, 2024[24]). Issuing floating rate bonds can help increase investor demand, and thereby liquidity, for a security since it offers investors positive exposure to higher interest rates if broader market conditions change, limiting the risk of being locked into lower than currently prevailing rates. However, from an issuer perspective it also increases the exposure to rate hikes which would lead to increased debt servicing costs. These risks can be addressed with hedging instruments, but these carry additional costs for the issuer. From a broader economic perspective, a high share of (unhedged) floating rate debt can also have financial stability implications. If debt servicing costs become unsustainable for a large enough number of companies, it may put upward pressure on default levels.

Figure 2.10. Split between floating and fixed rate bonds over time

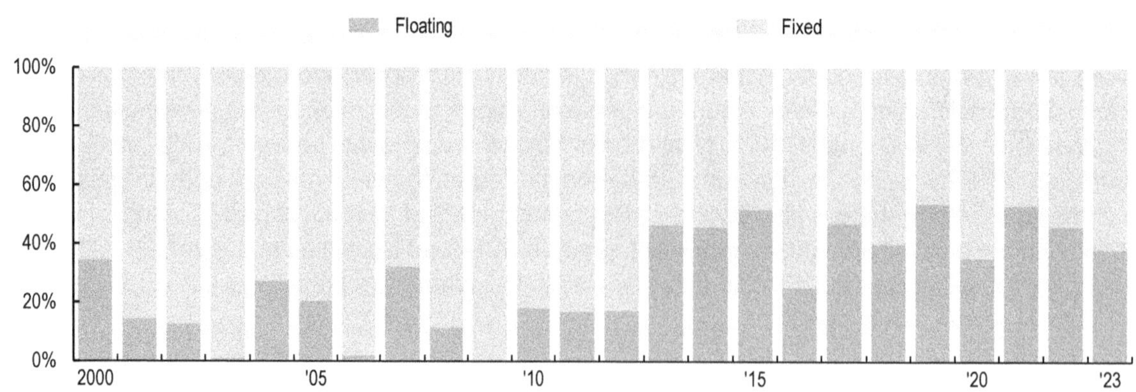

Note: By amount issued.
Source: OECD Capital Market Series dataset, LSEG, see Annex for details.

2.4. Issuer characteristics

In addition to market-level developments, it is useful to consider changes at the issuer level. Figure 2.11 below provides an overview of the composition of issuers on the Swedish bond market during the past two decades.

Before the global financial crisis, the corporate bond market in Sweden was clearly dominated by large companies issuing significant amounts. As with many of the trends shown thus far, there is a clear change after the 2008 financial crisis, and in particular after 2010. As shown in Panel A, both the median size of issuers and issues grew between early the 2000s and 2010. After that, both issuer and issue sizes have been declining. Panel B classifies issuers into three groups depending on their previous experience with bond markets: first-time issuers are issuers that have never issued a bond before; returning issuers has previously issued bonds, but more than five years ago; and active issuers have issued at least one bond within the last five years. Between 2000 and 2010, the average share of active issuers was 63% with first-time issuers representing 23%. On average, there were only eight issuers per year. In sharp contrast, the share of first-time issuers averaged 35% between 2011 and 2023, with an average of 41 issuers annually. In 2020, the number of issuers dropped sharply and the market was dominated by active issuers. In 2021 a record 73 companies issued bonds. However, similar to the dynamics seen in 2020, this number fell sharply in 2022 as market conditions grew less accommodative, with active issuers once more dominating.

Panel C shows the corresponding change in the distribution of issue sizes. Similarly, up until 2009 the market was clearly dominated by large companies. Issues larger than USD 500 million represented as much as a third of issues between 2000 and 2010. In 2007 it was as high as 62%. The two smaller categories below USD 100 million made up no more than 7% on average during this period. The dominance of large companies was particularly evident during the 2008 financial crisis when only very large and creditworthy Swedish companies had access to this type of market-based financing (Panel A). This led to a remarkably high median issue size, which peaked at USD 708 million in 2009 – higher than recorded in either Europe or the United States during the same period (OECD, 2021[6]). This dropped sharply after 2010, reaching USD 71 million in 2023, a decrease of around 80% compared to roughly a decade earlier. In the same year, issues below USD 100 million made up 71% of total issuance while the largest category (above USD 500 million) only represented 5%.

Figure 2.11. Characteristics of issuers/issues on the Swedish non-financial corporate bond market

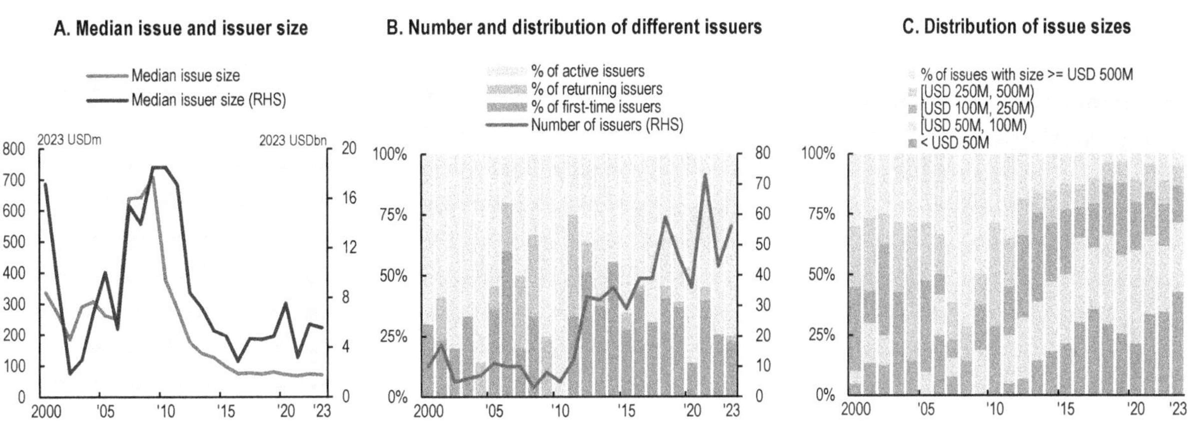

Note: Issuer size is defined as total assets. A company is defined as a first-time issuer if its bond issue in a given year is its first issue since the start of the data series (January 1980). A "returning issuer" is a company which made its last bond issue more than five years ago. If the company issued bonds in at least one of the past five years, it is defined as an "active issuer".
Source: OECD Capital Market Series dataset, LSEG, see Annex for details.

The increase in the number of issuers and general broadening of the market is also reflected in the concentration of issuers. Figure 2.12 below shows the share of the top three, five and ten largest issuers in total issuance over time. The share of the ten largest issuers has fallen sharply over the past decade, from an average of 78% in the period from 2011-2016 to 64% in the period from 2017-2023, with the three largest issuers' share falling from 39% to 35% in the same period. Notably, as an effect of tightening financial conditions, in both 2020 and 2022 the share of the ten largest issuers increased to 73% and 75% respectively, similar to the levels seen back in 2012. This follows from the sharp decrease in the number of issuers in these years, as shown in Figure 2.11. Within the investment grade category of the Swedish bond market, in 2020 only one of 132 issues came from a new issuer (Nordic Trustee, 2020[25]).

Figure 2.12. Largest issuers' share in total issuance

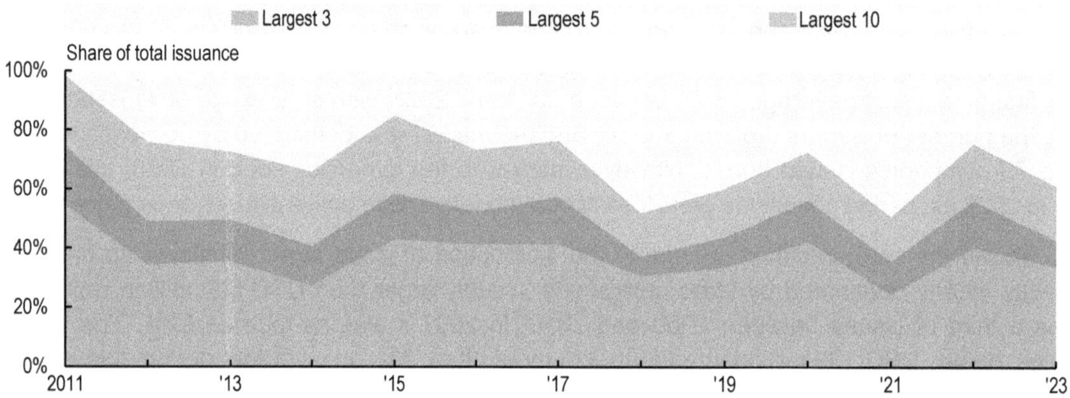

Note: 2011 is used as the starting point since the average number of annual issuers prior to that was no more than 8. In the period from 2011 to 2022, the annual average number of issuers was 40, with a peak of 73 issuers in 2021.
Source: OECD Capital Market Series dataset, LSEG, see Annex for details.

As the market has grown, its industry composition has changed. However, despite significant variation between years, certain industries have remained dominant. Notably, industrial companies make up a substantial share of the total amount issued through corporate bonds throughout the analysed period, averaging 27% of annual issuance from 2000 to 2023, and reaching as much as 38% during the last three years. Consumer cyclicals, utility and telecom are also large issuers (Figure 2.13).

It should be noted that bonds issued by real estate companies are not included here. A separate section (2.9) is devoted to an analysis of the real estate sector. More generally, it bears mentioning that the financial industry, which is not considered in this report, represents a significant share of the Swedish bond market, accounting for as much as 73% of total issuance in 2023.

Figure 2.13. Industry composition of the Swedish non-financial bond market

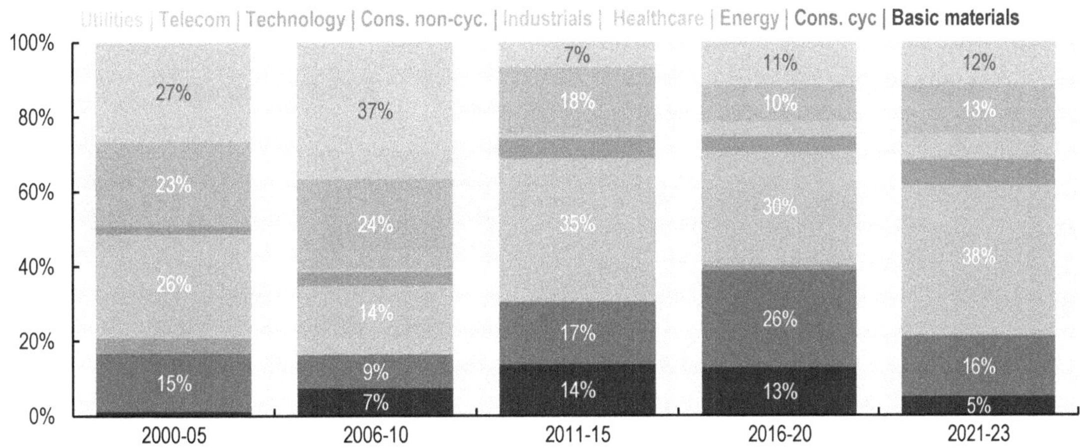

Note: Shares in total issuance for each period. Real estate companies are not considered in the above graph. Refer to section 2.9 for an analysis including the real estate industry.
Source: OECD Capital Market Series dataset, LSEG, see Annex for details.

2.5. Corporate bond investors

Foreign investors are the largest owners of Swedish non-financial corporate bonds. By the end of Q3-2023 they held 63% of the total outstanding amount. This share has remained quite stable since 2003. The composition of domestic ownership, however, has changed. An important development is the growth of investment funds as owners since about 2012. In 2011, they held about 2% of total outstanding amounts, a figure that had grown to 14% by Q3-2023 (Figure 2.14, Panel A). Their portion of domestic ownership represents 39%, compared to 6% in 2011 (Panel B). The use of aggregate statistics does not allow for a breakdown of the foreign investor category. However, this is also likely to include a substantial amount of investment funds (Becker et al., 2020[26]).

Monetary financial institutions (MFIs, e.g. banks, money market funds and other credit institutions) represent 13% of domestic ownership, a decrease from 46% in 2009. This is significant and reflects the overhaul of the regulatory landscape, in particular for banks, after the 2008 financial crisis, notably the new Basel accords. Higher capital and liquidity requirements for banks have made it increasingly capital-intensive to hold inventories of corporate bonds. This has led to a reduction in proprietary inventories and a decrease in dealer intermediation (FSB, 2021[27]). Non-financial companies themselves represent 7% of domestic ownership of non-financial bonds. Direct retail (household) participation in bond markets is very low, but retail investors are still exposed to the market through e.g. investment and pension funds.

Figure 2.14. Ownership structure of outstanding Swedish non-financial bonds

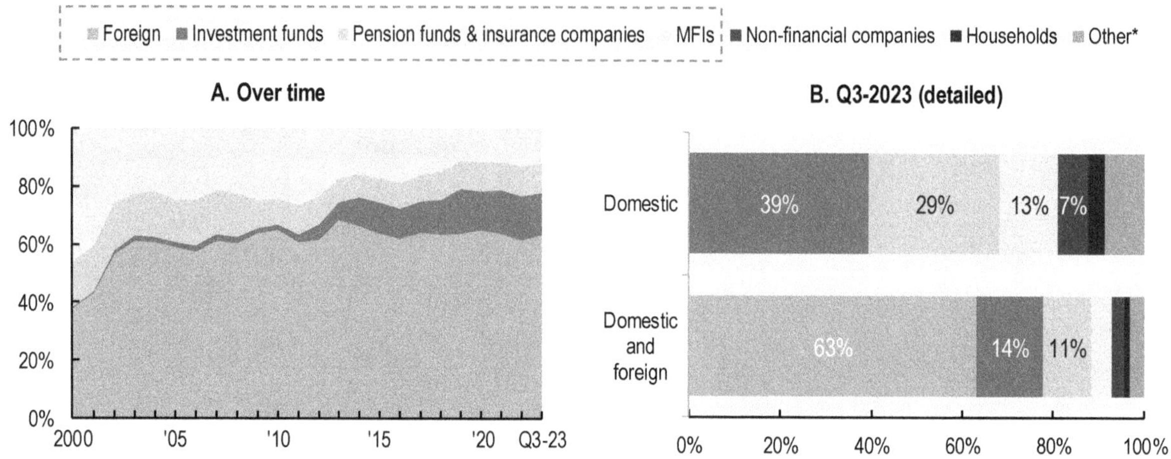

Note: In Panel B, the "Other" category includes: the Swedish central bank, public administration and other financial intermediaries (original classification in raw data). In Panel A, the "Other" category includes all of these, plus those shown in Panel B but not in Panel A (non-financial companies and households). Data refer only to corporate bonds (not short-term securities). All values are as of year-end except 2023.
Source: Financial Accounts from Statistics Sweden (SCB).

2.6. Covenant protection

Covenants are constraints placed on an issuer and are stipulated in the bond indenture (contract) at the time of issuance. They are bondholders' main corporate governance tool and serve to ensure that issuers do not engage in activities that would reduce creditors' claims or reduce the probability that they are repaid. A breach of covenant will give the bondholders certain legal remedies specified in the indenture, often to accelerate the bonds. Previous OECD analysis (2021[6]) has shown a clear decrease in covenant protection over time for non-investment grade bonds issued in the United States.

The availability of covenant data for Swedish non-financial bonds through commercial databases is very limited, making it difficult to provide an assessment of developments over time. Based on available data, Figure 2.15 shows how the prevalence of certain covenants in Swedish bond indentures has changed over time, by comparing two nine-year periods. While incomplete, certain trends are visible. For example, the prevalence of negative pledge covenants, preventing issuers from using encumbered assets as collateral for new borrowing (which would dilute the existing creditors' protection), has decreased markedly over time. Contrarily, change of control covenants – under which a material change in a corporate ownership (definitions may vary) would trigger an obligation to repay the outstanding debt – have become much more common. The same is true for *pari passu* covenants, which are meant to guarantee that existing creditors are covered by potential additional guarantees the issuer offers to creditors in future borrowing. However, it should be noted that there are substantial differences in the prevalence of different covenants between consecutive years, making it difficult to determine the exact trends. Several market participants have suggested the commercially available data do not reflect their understanding of market trends, noting that e.g. negative pledge and cross default provisions are present in the vast majority of issues. These data can thus be interpreted primarily as an indication of a lack of readily available information.

Figure 2.15. Prevalence of different covenants in Swedish non-financial bond indentures

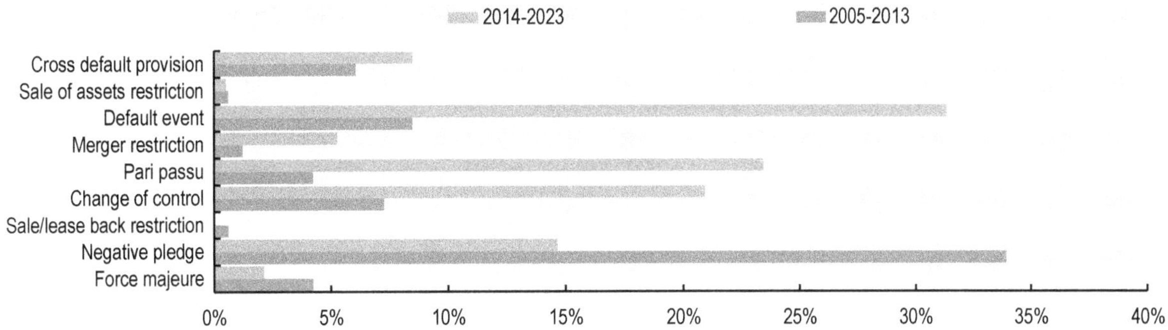

Note: There are significant data availability restrictions for covenants on Swedish non-financial bonds. This figure should be interpreted considering this limitation. It is based on 1 171 bonds issued by Swedish non-financial companies between 2000 and 2023 with covenant indicators available. Only covenants that are included in at least one bond indenture are displayed.
Source: OECD Capital Market Series dataset, LSEG, see Annex for details.

2.7. Investment banks and market structure

Investment banks play important roles in corporate bond markets, providing underwriting and advisory services. Their services are related to e.g. origination, distribution, risk bearing and certification, as well as advice on pricing, timing of issuance and preparation of relevant documentation. As a general trend, the market concentration of investment banks underwriting non-financial bonds in Sweden has decreased somewhat in the past decade, although the trajectory has been uneven. In 2023, the top five banks had a market share of 67%, compared to 73% in 2010 (Figure 2.16, Panel A). In 2023, all of the top five banks by market share were Swedish or Nordic (Panel B). This is a relatively recent phenomenon. While local banks were always relatively high up in the league tables, up until 2017 the top five always included, and was often dominated by, foreign banks, notably from the United States, the United Kingdom, Germany and France. This increase in the share of local investment banks can also be observed in other regions, notably in a number of Asian jurisdictions (OECD, 2019[28]).

Figure 2.16. Composition of underwriters of non-financial bonds

A. Market share of top 5 banks in each year

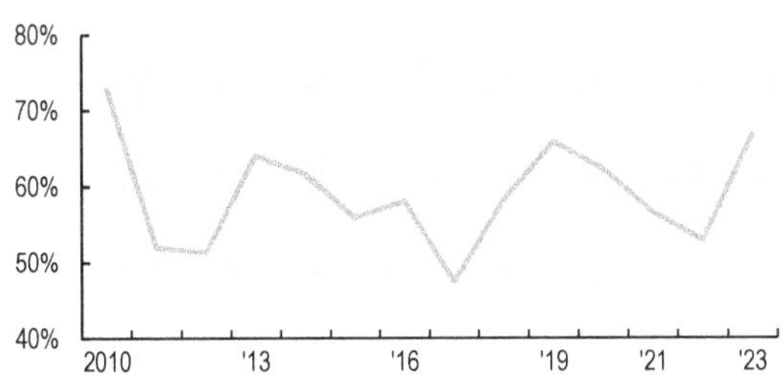

B. Top 5 banks in 2023

Bank	Mkt share
Danske Bank	16%
SEB	15%
Nordea	15%
Handelsbanken Capital Markets	14%
Swedbank	7%
Top 5 market share	**67%**

Note: Ranked based on gross proceeds. Panel A shows the share of the top five banks in any given year. However, the composition of the top five differs over time, meaning there can be changes in which banks are included.
Source: LSEG.

When a bond is issued, the issuer normally assigns an independent trustee to supervise the implementation of the bond indenture (contract), in Sweden called an agent. The role of the agent, typically a bank or a specialised institution, is to ensure the contract is followed, including to review instances of covenant breaches, and to handle communication between bondholders and the issuer, as well as to manage bondholder meetings, when held.[10] In terms of specialised agent institutions, the Swedish market is dominated by two main players, Nordic Trustee and Intertrust, and by the former in particular. In many markets, the agent/trustee often also plays the role of paying agent, handling collection and disbursements of principal and coupon payments. This is also the case in Nordic markets such as Norway. In Sweden, however, there are no paying agents. Instead, disbursements to bondholders are typically handled by the central securities depository, generally Euroclear (which only provides settlements in euros and Swedish krona). It also bears mentioning that the role of the agent is not specifically regulated, which is the case in, for instance, Finland, Denmark and Norway, as well as in the United States and the United Kingdom through fiduciary duties.[11]

Based on bond issues for which agent information were available between 2012–2023, Figure 2.17 provides an overview of agents active in the Swedish market. By number of transactions, specialised and independent agents – notably Nordic Trustee – dominate the market. Looking at transaction amounts, banks supplying agent services are more prevalent, due to the larger average size of investment grade bonds for which banks more often play the role of agent.

Figure 2.17. Agents on the Swedish bond market, 2012-2023

A. Market share by agent type

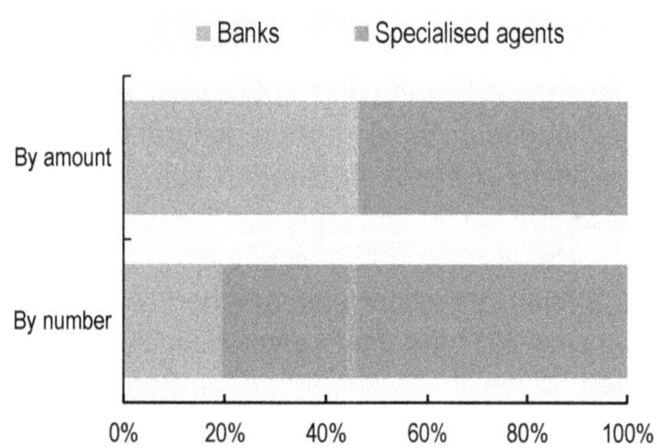

B. Top 5 agents

By number of transactions	By amount
1. Nordic Trustee	1. Deutsche Bank
2. Intertrust	2. Nordic Trustee
3. Deutsche Bank	3. Intertrust
4. Citibank	4. Citibank
5. US Bank Trustees	5. US Bank Trustees

Note: Based on 356 deals by non-financial companies (excluding the real estate sector) domiciled in Sweden between 2012-2023 for which agent information is available. Cases where the agent was not defined (labelled "Other Trustees") have been excluded.
Source: Nordic Trustee.

2.8. Secondary market liquidity

A liquid secondary market is an important aspect of all market-based financing, facilitating efficient price discovery and enabling investors to enter and exit at any given time, thus also supporting the primary market.

Generally, liquidity is significantly lower on corporate bond markets than on equity markets. Partly, this has to do with the nature of the instrument. For many investors, bonds serve the purpose of long-term liability matching, making it a suitable instrument for institutional investors with long-term portfolio structures. This reduces liquidity, since the largest investor categories are not liquidity suppliers but rather liquidity takers through buy-and-hold strategies. Trading in corporate bonds is typically concentrated in a short period after a bond is issued, following which it drops significantly. Evidence from the US market suggests that most trading takes place in the first 90 days after issuance (Mizrach, 2015[29]). Moreover, the vast majority of outstanding bonds do not trade on any given day. Even for the most traded bonds, the number of trades per day is limited (Çelik, Demirtaş and Isaksson, 2015[30]).

Low liquidity also has to do with trading mechanisms. As opposed to equities, bonds are typically traded in large increments. For example, in the United States the average bond trade size from 2014-16 was

USD 1.2 million. This is compared to an estimated USD 3 000 to 5 000 for equities, less than 0.5% of the size of an average bond trade (Bessembinder, Spatt and Venkataraman, 2020[31]). Similarly, in 2022 the average corporate bond trade size in the secondary market in the EU and UK was EUR 829 000 (ICMA, 2022[32]). This is because most bond markets target large institutional investors, who trade in large minimum sizes. The retail component of the market (at least for direct investments) is typically small. In addition, electronic trading, although increasing, makes up a relatively small part of the market. Phone-based negotiations remain dominant, in particular for larger bonds, in sharp contrast to equity markets where electronic trading is ubiquitous (FSB, 2021[27]).

Finally, bond market trading has historically been dominated by dealer intermediation by banks, which therefore play an important part in creating liquidity. In 2014, 95% of secondary market trading in Sweden was made up by trading between banks and their customers (Riksbanken, 2014[21]). However, in many places the growth in bond dealer balance sheets has not matched the growth of the corporate bond market. In addition, partly following more stringent regulation in the wake of the 2008 financial crisis as well as increased risk aversion, banks hold smaller inventories of bonds and have reduced their activities as market makers, further reducing liquidity. Riskless principal trading – where the dealer finds both a buyer and a seller before going ahead with a trade – is now a more common business model than regular principal trading (FSB, 2021[27]).

In recent years, the annual volume traded on the Swedish market has slightly outpaced the growth of the market more broadly. Figure 2.18 provides an overview of annual volumes of Swedish non-financial corporate bonds traded on the secondary market and the turnover ratio (measured as annual traded volumes as a share of the outstanding amount at the end of the year). Trading volumes generally increased up until 2021, after which there has been a notable decrease. The Swedish turnover ratio is lower than the European aggregate. In the European Economic Area (excluding the United Kingdom), the turnover ratio in 2020 was 46%, compared to an average of 32% in Sweden from 2019-23 (ESMA, 2021[33]). It should be noted, however, that the Swedish Riksbank's statistics on corporate bond turnover refers only to bonds denominated in Swedish crowns. This may understate the aggregate market liquidity, given the significantly larger size of the average Swedish foreign currency denominated bond (see Figure 3.5).

Figure 2.18. Turnover in the secondary corporate bond market

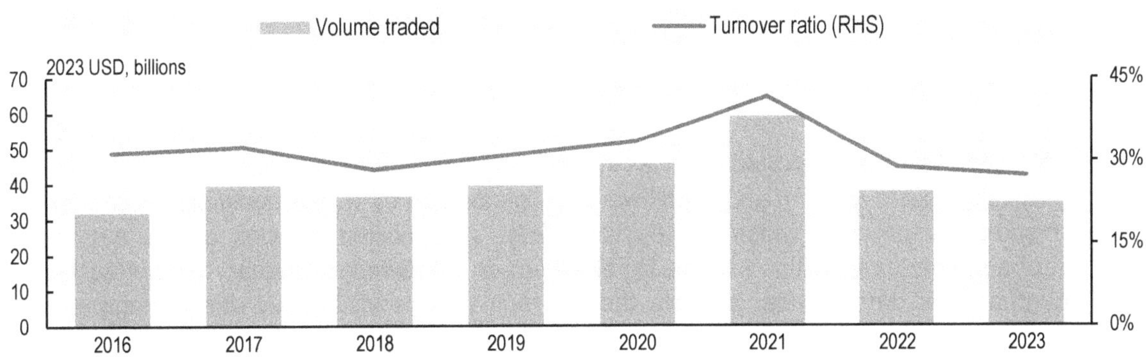

Note: Refers to SEK-denominated non-financial corporate bonds. The turnover ratio is calculated as the annual traded volume as a share of the outstanding amount of corporate bonds at the end of the year. See endnotes for commentary on data used in this figure.
Source: Sveriges Riksbank (SELMA Statistics), OECD Capital Market Series dataset, LSEG.

According to Wollert (2020[13]), a lack of transparency in pricing and trading has led to unreliable pricing in the Swedish market. Analysis by the Swedish Financial Supervisory Authority has shown that part of this reduction in transparency has been a result of implementing the European Union's directive MiFID II and MiFIR in 2018. Prior to its implementation all bond trades, with the exception of trades exceeding SEK 50 million, had to be disclosed no later than 09.00 (AM) the following day. MIFiD II and MiFIR have, on the face of it, more stringent disclosure requirements, mandating such disclosure both pre-trade (orders) and post-trade (transactions) effectively in real time. For pre-trade disclosure, the main rule states that buy and sell bids as well as order depth should be disclosed continuously by market operators and investment firms operating a trading venue during market hours.[12] However, due to waivers included in the directive, all investment firms trading in Swedish bonds are exempt from pre-trade disclosure (it should be noted that pre-trade transparency was very low also prior to the implementation of MiFIR). When it comes to post-trade disclosure, MiFIR lists three conditions under which disclosure of non-equity transactions may be deferred. They apply to transactions that are: 1) larger than normal market size; 2) related to instruments for which there is no liquid market; or 3) above an instrument-specific size. For trades subject to deferrals based on these criteria, information is to be disclosed at latest 19:00 (7:00 PM) the second working day after the trade. In practice, since only a handful of Swedish bonds are considered liquid under this regulation, essentially all trades are eligible for deferrals. In August 2019, only one Swedish ISIN bond was considered liquid. The effect of this has been reduced transparency on the Swedish bond markets. According to a survey of market participants, well above 60% find that MiFID II/MiFIR has decreased transparency, with just under 30% saying it is unchanged (Finansinspektionen, 2019[34]).[13]

The Financial Supervisory Authority's analysis further shows that the reduced transparency is due to fragmentation in data provision (such as turnover data, which was previously available in one place), caused by the lack of one entity compiling all published information (a "consolidated tape provider" or CTP). However, as part of the MiFIR/D II review, there is now political agreement at the EU level for an EU-wide consolidated tape, which includes post-trade data for bonds (European Commission, 2023[8]).

In line with the objectives of MiFIR/MiFID II, trading on regulated venues has increased. Before their implementation in 2018, effectively all Swedish corporate bonds were traded OTC. By 2019 the OTC trading had fallen to below 40% while trading on regulated venues has increased. Much of this increase refers to systematic internalisers (executing orders against their own books or client orders), but increases can also be seen on trading venues including regulated markets, MTFs and OTFs.[14] Data show that in practice, transactions executed by systematic internalisers are published two days after the trade. For transactions executed on an MTF, the delay is normally four weeks or more for all types of bonds, although in Sweden this deferral only applies to sovereign and covered bonds and not for corporate bonds. However, most MTF trades in Swedish corporate bonds are executed on platforms that fall under other EU country regulations. Different jurisdictions apply different waivers, and the Swedish FSA has found discrepancies between the transaction data it receives and the publicly available data, meaning the latter gives an incomplete view of the market (Finansinspektionen, 2019[34]). It remains to be evaluated what the effect of the MiFIR/D II revision will be on market transparency.

In response to their findings, in 2020 the Swedish Financial Supervisory Authority tasked the Swedish Securities Markets Association (SSMA) with examining ways to improve transparency. As a result, the mandatory rules set out in MiFID II and MiFIR were complemented by a self-regulatory recommendation on bond market transparency, which applies voluntarily. The recommendation entails e.g. the daily publication of aggregate transaction information executed on the Swedish market, which is to be made public through a single data provider. Notably, the self-regulatory provisions are more stringent than the mandatory national rules applied prior to the implementation of the EU directive (Swedish Securities Markets Association, 2020[35]). Survey results evaluating the self-regulatory approach indicate that it has had a positive effect on transparency.

It bears mentioning that while increased transparency in bond markets is generally beneficial to liquidity, a balance needs to be struck between transparency and dealer incentives to intermediate. Typically, if a trade leads a dealer to add bonds to its inventory, it will want to resell these bonds in the inter-dealer market. Forcing dealers to show their hand in terms of inventory may compromise their bargaining position in that market, in turn reducing their incentives to intermediate. This is particularly pertinent for high-yield, illiquid bonds (Çelik, Demirtaş and Isaksson, 2015[30]). However, it is difficult to establish which way the causality runs. Limited transparency may be required to maintain dealer incentives for markets with low liquidity, but low liquidity may equally be an effect of low transparency.

While corporate bonds are typically traded OTC, in certain markets they trade primarily on-exchange, similar to equities. This model is applied for example in the Israeli and Chilean markets. With respect to the Israeli market, some research has found that these features encourage retail investors[15] to participate more actively in corporate bond trading and contribute to increased liquidity. Notably, retail investors account for 8.8% of the double-sided volume traded in Israel (Abudym and Wohl, 2018[36]). In 2021, the on-exchange traded volume on the Tel Aviv Stock Exchange (TASE) was USD 56 billion, compared to USD 1 billion off-exchange, meaning more than 98% of the volume traded of corporate bonds took place on-exchange (TASE, 2022[37]). TASE has 24 members, consisting of banks and brokers, who can connect directly to the TASE trading system. An investor, i.e. TASE member clients, can submit orders online and check the status and the order book. Unlike OTC trading, the accessibility and transparency offered by the exchange allows retail investors with small investments to participate in the corporate bond market, which in most countries is accessible only to institutional and qualified investors.

Similarly, in Chile, although the market is only open to qualified investors, corporate bonds trade on the Santiago Stock Exchange (BCS) through two open systems. The first system, called TELERENTA, automatically matches buy and sell orders through a continuous order book, giving priority to the lowest market-clearing price (BCS, 2016[38]). The second system, also operated by the exchange, is a periodic English Auction system. Like in Israel, on-exchange transactions make up the lion's share of trading, accounting for 75% of all traded volume in 2022 (BCS[39]).

While on-exchange trading systems may have important benefits in terms of broadened access to the bond market (notably for retail investors) and in terms of reduced spreads, it is not evident that it is beneficial to liquidity (measured as turnover). From 2019 to 2021, the average turnover for corporate bonds on TASE was 49%, similar to the levels in the EEA (excluding the UK) (TASE[40]).

2.8.1. The Swedish corporate bond market during COVID-19

This subsection provides an overview of the dynamics of the Swedish corporate bond market during the COVID-19 crisis, including subsequent initiatives to improve market functioning, both from regulators and private sector representatives.

Well-functioning capital markets serve to provide an economy with increased resilience in times of crisis, allowing companies to access financing even as risk aversion increases, typically resulting in contractions in both bank credit and consumer demand, simultaneously increasing the need for financing and decreasing the availability of capital. In 2009, non-financial companies globally issued record amounts of bonds, and the same dynamics played out in 2020 at the onset of the pandemic. The same pattern can be seen for equity markets (secondary public offerings, i.e. already listed companies tapping equity markets, are of particular importance) (OECD, 2021[6]). These developments are indicative of the ability of market-based financing to help economies overcome periods of financial and general economic distress. However, a prerequisite for this is that markets are sufficiently flexible, liquid and deep. When they are not, they offer less resilience in times of crises.

Figure 2.19 shows net credit flows to Swedish non-financial companies over time. Panel A illustrates the same broader Swedish trend seen in previous figures, namely a shift from bank financing towards debt securities around 2011. It also gives an indication of the pro- or counter-cyclicality of different types of borrowing during crises. In 2009, as bank lending contracted sharply, debt security issuance actually increased. However, two points need to be considered when interpreting these data. First, the year after, in 2010, credit flows from debt securities contracted more than bank loans in absolute terms, despite being a much smaller market segment. Second, the Swedish bond market of 2009 was very different from the one of today. As illustrated in Figure 2.11, in those years the market was dominated by a small number of large, established issuers issuing significant amounts. While market access for such companies is indeed important, it is not necessarily a good indicator of the extent to which a market provides resilience more broadly. The COVID-19 crisis provides a better test of this, since by 2020 the market had expanded significantly to include a larger number of companies. Panel B below shows quarterly net credit flows from 2020 to 2023. Notably, it shows debt securities contracting in the second quarter of 2020 during the peak of the pandemic-related market uncertainty. These flows turned positive again in the third quarter, notably as the Riksbank's corporate bond purchasing programme began in September, instilling a degree of trust in the continued functioning of the market.

Figure 2.19. Net credit flows to non-financial companies in Sweden

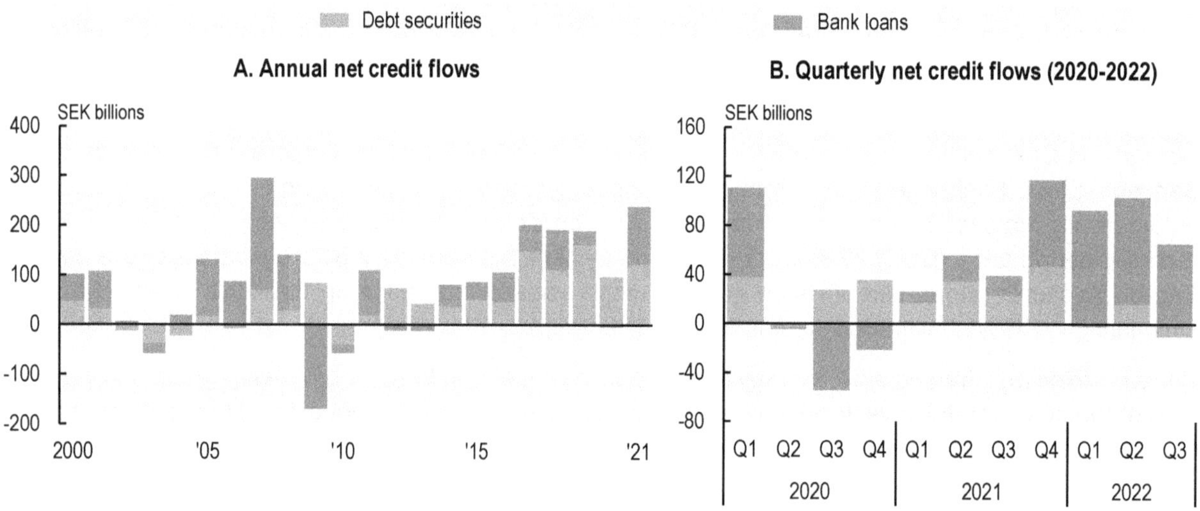

Note: See endnotes for commentary on data updates relating to this figure.
Source: Financial Accounts from Statistics Sweden (SCB).

Figure 2.20 provides a more detailed account of primary market issuance during the COVID-19 crisis. In the early months of the pandemic, issuance was significantly lower than its five-year average for the market as a whole (Panel A). With the exception of July and September (when the central bank's purchasing programme began and issuance increased sharply), this held true for the full year. February and November saw similar numbers as previous years. This is in sharp contrast to global developments, where total issuance markedly exceeded historical averages, in particular in the crucial months of March, April, May and June (OECD, 2021[6]). To an extent, this is likely driven by the US Federal Reserve's intervention in March 2020, which was much earlier than the Swedish equivalent.

However, as Panels B and C reveal, the dynamics differed substantially between the investment grade and non-investment grade segments of the Swedish market. Notably, investment grade issuance was in line with previous years' issuance for the full year, and significantly higher in February, September and November. Total issuance in 2020 was 63% higher than in 2019. Contrarily, non-investment grade issuance was non-existent in the first three months of 2020. It remained below historical averages in every month, with the exception of April, July and September. However, issuance in these months was driven by a handful of large bonds by no more than one issuer per month.[16] In total in 2020, there were no more than five non-investment grade bonds issued by Swedish companies, and the full-year amount was 24% lower than historical averages.

Figure 2.20. Swedish non-financial bond issuances during the COVID-19 pandemic

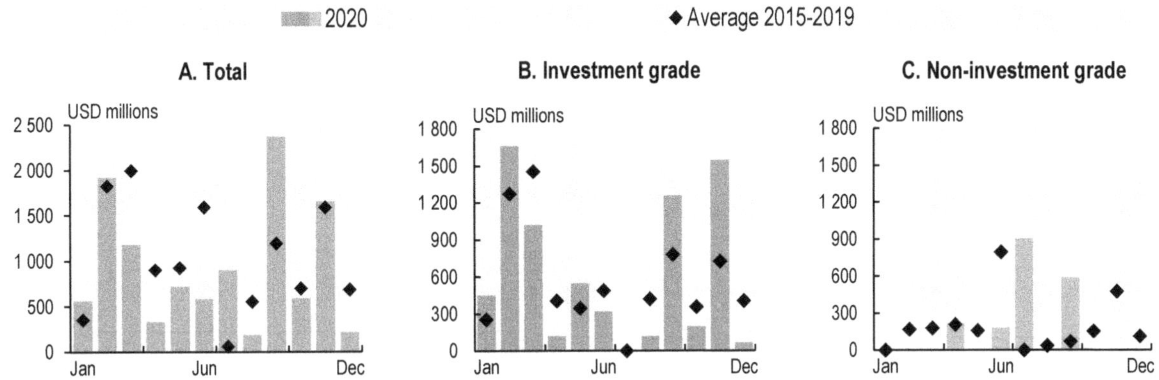

Note: Panel A includes unrated bonds. Not adjusted for inflation.
Source: OECD Capital Market Series dataset, LSEG, see Annex for details.

The significant impact of the COVID-19 crisis can be seen even more clearly in the secondary market. Figure 2.21 below shows how an index of investment grade bonds issued in SEK developed during 2020 and more recently. The index fell very sharply in March 2020, gradually recovering over the year, assisted by significant fiscal and monetary support at the national and supranational levels (Panel A). Panel B shows the option-adjusted spread, which increased 2.5 times from 31 January to 24 March. These developments are both indicative of a major sell-off and liquidity crunch. These dynamics were not unique to Sweden. The S&P 500 Investment Grade Corporate Bond Index (effectively the US equivalent of the index presented below) fell even deeper and spreads increased more than for the Swedish index. However, this should be considered with two points in mind. Firstly, substantial parts of the Swedish market are unrated (as seen in Figure 2.4) or rated non-investment grade. Since the index does not reflect these bonds, it gives only a partial picture of the market which is likely skewed towards its strongest part. Secondly, the US index recovered much faster (both in terms of performance and spread) and more strongly after the initial downturn, indicating less uncertainty about the market's continued functioning (again aided by substantial fiscal/monetary support). In addition, the figure illustrates the significant pressure the market has been subject to with the tightening of monetary policy since 2022, with valuations falling below the 2020 nadir and spreads reaching similar levels. Comparable developments can be seen globally, although Swedish spreads appear to be very elevated compared to e.g. the S&P 500 index mentioned above, for which spreads did not come close to reaching 2020 levels in 2022.

During the COVID-induced crisis, a lack of liquidity was arguably the most pressing issue on the Swedish corporate bond market. During times of financial distress, supply and demand on capital markets tend to be lopsided as large parts of the market rush to sell riskier assets and to buy safe ones. These dynamics lead to e.g. the increased spread seen in the market, typically coupled with a widened bid-ask spread for most corporate bonds. However, in a resilient market, the price formation process should not break down entirely in such a scenario. When it does, it is indicative of a completely one-sided market where prospective sellers are not certain they will be able to find a buyer at all for their investments. These tendencies were visible in the Swedish bond markets in 2020 (and indeed in Europe more generally), as roughly 30 investment funds, with aggregate assets under management equivalent to some SEK 120 billion, temporarily froze owing to lacking information on closing prices and trading volume (Riksbanken, 2021[41]). In addition to domestic investment funds, foreign investors also offloaded significant holdings of Swedish corporate bonds (Becker et al., 2020[26]).

Figure 2.21. S&P Sweden 1+ Year Investment Grade Corporate Bond Index

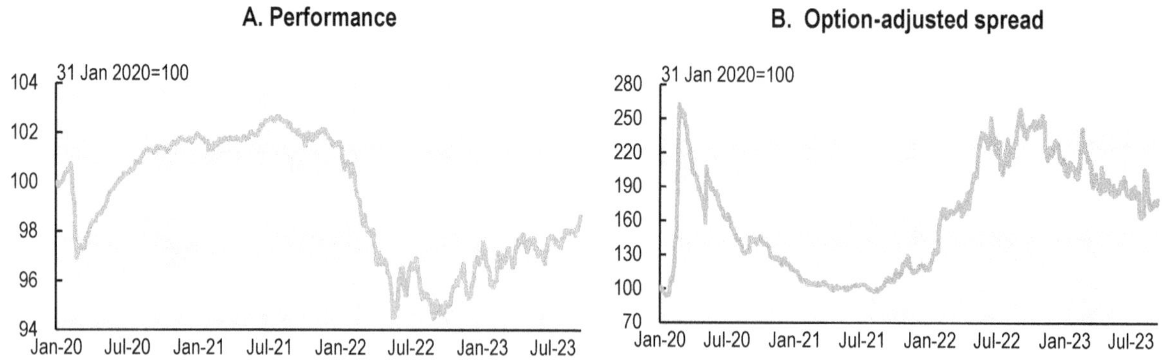

Note: The index includes investment grade bonds (as determined by ratings from S&P, Moody's or Fitch) denominated in SEK with a minimum notional outstanding amount of SEK 250 million and a maturity of more than one year.
Source: S&P Global.

These adverse developments were to an extent an effect of the ownership structure on the Swedish market. As shown in Figure 2.14, investment funds represent a significant share of domestic ownership. Similar to banks, open-ended investment funds engage in liquidity transformation, since they offer investors share liquidity which exceeds that of the underlying assets. There is evidence that in the EU as a whole, the share of non-liquid assets in bond funds' total assets has increased substantially over time (ESRB, 2019[42]). The potential threat of this type of activity to financial stability is typically not visible as long as there is not a significant demand from investors to liquidate their assets simultaneously. This is, however, precisely what happened during the COVID-19 crisis. Panel A of Figure 2.22 shows how market turnover increased over historical averages, roughly doubling in February and March of 2020. Panel B shows the Riksbank's share in total secondary market turnover, following its intervention in the markets. It should be noted that these increases are not indicative of improved general liquidity, since they do not take account of the increased selling pressure (i.e. they do not say anything about the development of the share of trades that could not – at least not at a price deemed acceptable to the seller – be executed), nor of the difference between types of bonds (e.g. investment grade and non-investment grade).

Figure 2.22. Turnover in the Swedish secondary corporate bond market during the COVID-19 pandemic

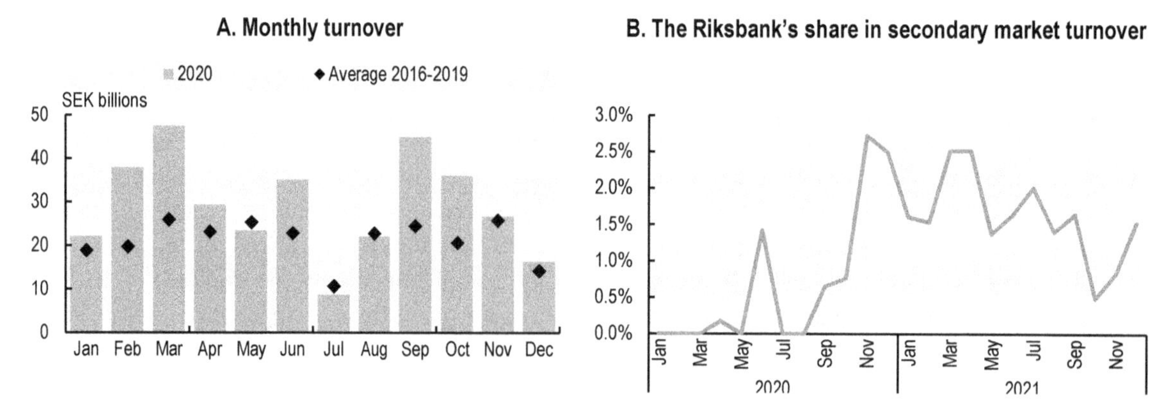

Note: Refers to spot contracts for SEK-denominated corporate bonds. Monthly figures are sums of daily data. Secondary market trading is calculated as total turnover subtracted by transactions identified as primary market trading. See endnotes for commentary on data used in this figure.
Source: Sveriges Riksbank (SELMA Statistics).

The FSA's analysis concludes that the corporate bond market has not offered more flexible financing than banks in times of crises in Sweden, meaning it does not provide the same type of counter-cyclical financing as the EU and US markets. However, issuers who could access bond markets in foreign currencies were able to benefit from greater flexibility. Over the past decade, the vast majority of SEK denominated bonds issued by Swedish companies (around 90%) were not traded on any given day, compared to a figure of about 60% for foreign currency denominated bonds. However, it bears mentioning that Sweden has a stable and profitable banking system that exited the 2008 financial crisis (and the subsequent euro crisis) in a comparatively strong position. Notably, while bank lending was below trend in Sweden both following 2008 and the euro crisis, this was driven by a decrease in foreign currency lending, whereas domestic currency bank loans remained remarkably stable (Becker et al., 2020[26]).

2.8.2. Policy responses to improve market resilience and liquidity

Shortcomings in the Swedish bond market during the COVID-19 crisis have prompted initiatives by several regulators and public bodies to reform the market and increase its resilience. Notably, in 2021 the government tasked the FSA with investigating the need for additional liquidity management tools to deal with liquidity risk for investment funds. It reviewed three such tools: *swing pricing* (adjusting the fund unit value or sales and redemption price of the units up/down depending on the costs associated with the fund's net flows); *anti-dilution levies* (a fee levied on investors when they sell/redeem fund units); and *redemption gates* (allowing funds to postpone redemptions above pre-defined thresholds). The FSA's assessment was that the application of anti-dilutions levies is possible within the existing legal framework, along with a certain type of swing pricing.[17] It also believes that the use of redemption gates should be allowed. The conditions for applying these tools should be regulated "in legislation and related regulations". Swing pricing has been identified as a priority area. The FSA also recommends that a requirement for investment funds to be open for redemption at least twice per month be reflected in law, along with the longest allowed redemption time (Finansinspektionen, 2021[43]).

In an article in the financial press, the Director General of the FSA has also urged market participants to improve their conduct, notably with respect to disclosure and transparency, and encouraged the development of a self-regulatory regime by the SSMA. The article stresses the need for investment funds to improve their liquidity management by designing their portfolios with scenarios of market pressure in mind, for example increasing the share of liquid assets or making clear to investors that they do not offer daily redemptions (Finansinspektionen, 2021[14]). These discussions are reminiscent of those that took place in the United States during the so-called "taper tantrum" in mid-2013 when the substantial selling pressure had large effects on corporate bond prices and officials considered imposing exit fees on bond funds (Çelik, Demirtaş and Isaksson, 2015[30]).

Further, the Riksbank, the Swedish National Debt Office and the FSA have jointly called for the introduction of a Swedish standard for benchmark bonds. Their proposed benchmark standard has three key elements: a minimum issuance of SEK 1 billion (corresponding to roughly USD 100 million at the time of publication of the proposal – as shown in Figure 2.11, in 2023 more than 70% of the number of bonds issued by Swedish companies were below USD 100 million); a minimum of two bookrunners to broaden the investor base; and issued through syndicated public transactions in line with the Eurobond market standard. The institutions argue that this would help develop a base of long-term investors such as insurance companies and pension funds that contribute less to liquidity crunches in times of financial distress compared to the currently dominant investment funds. In addition, they suggest that moving towards a benchmark standard would increase liquidity in the market, to the benefit of e.g. investment funds that depend on liquid markets to meet redemptions (Finansinspektionen, 2022[15]).

Panel A of Figure 2.23 illustrates the total amount of existing issuance made up of bonds that comply with the proposed benchmark criteria and explores the extent to which this could be increased based on the existing market structure. Potential benchmark issues are identified in two different ways. The first refers to bonds that already have a denomination that is larger than or equal to SEK 1 billion but that use less than two bookrunners and/or are not syndicated. The second category instead looks at bonds with denominations below SEK 1 billion that are issued by companies that could reasonably issue benchmark standard bonds. These companies are defined as those whose total issuance, based on several bonds, exceeds SEK 1 billion over a one-year period. Only the small-in-size bonds by these issuers are considered in the amount of potential benchmark bonds. From 2005-2023, the total actual benchmark issuance by Swedish companies amounted to USD 163 billion (67% of total issuance during this period). Using the above provided definitions of potential benchmark issues suggests that an additional USD 56 billion could have been issued through benchmark bonds, an increase of over one-third, bringing the total to USD 219 billion (90% of total issuance). The potential benchmark amounts are roughly evenly split between bonds with a denomination above SEK 1 billion and small-in-size bonds issued by potential benchmark issuers. Since benchmark issues by definition are large in size, when looking at the number of bonds issued rather than amounts, benchmark bonds made up 23% of all issued bonds during the same period.

Panel B shows the share of benchmark issues in total issuance over time, which has fallen from an average of 77% from 2005-2010 to 64% from 2011-2023. This is in line with the broadening of the market to include smaller issuers.

Figure 2.23. Existing and potential Swedish benchmark issuance, 2005-2023

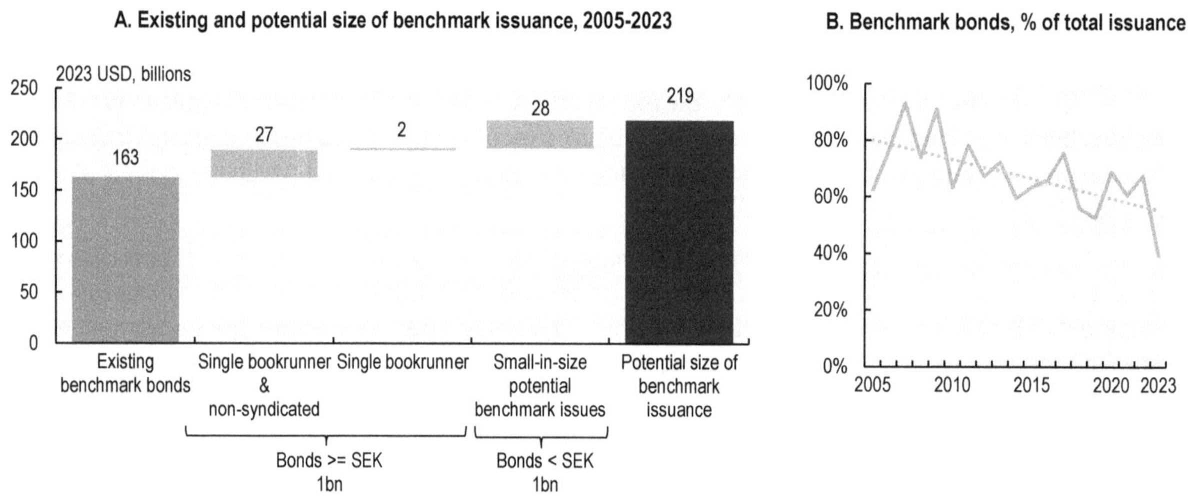

Note: Refers to non-financial companies. The definition of a benchmark issue is in line with the proposal by the Swedish Riksbank, the Financial Services Authority and the National Debt Office and is defined as any bond that: has an (inflation-adjusted) issuance amount above or equal to 1 billion SEK; a minimum of two bookrunners; and is syndicated. There are two categories of potential benchmark bonds. The first is bonds that already fulfil the size criterion (>= 1bn SEK), but that are not syndicated and/or use a single bookrunner. The second category is bonds that are smaller in size than SEK 1 billion but that are issued by a company that is identified as a potential benchmark issuer, defined as having issued at least SEK 1 billion and more than one bond in a one-year period. Only the small-in-size bonds by these issuers are considered in the amount of potential benchmark bonds.
Source: OECD Capital Market Series Dataset, LSEG.

In addition to encouraging the development of such a standard, the central bank has outlined a number of recommendations of measures that can be taken by different market participants, which are summarised in Box 2.1.

Box 2.1. The Riksbank's proposals for a better functioning corporate bond market

In its 2021 report *Towards a better functioning corporate bond market*, the Swedish Riksbank outlined a number of possible action points for different market participants (issuers, investors and banks). Its nine recommendations are briefly summarised below.

Issuers

Companies issuing bonds may contribute to market development and liquidity by: issuing fewer but larger bonds, thus establishing a credit curve; involving more banks (bookrunners/arrangers) in the issue process, thereby expanding the investor base; and obtaining credit ratings for more issues.

Investors

Investors, most notably investment funds, may: communicate more clearly to retail investors the liquidity risk and limitations of investing in fixed income funds (notably by reporting spread exposure[1] in fact sheets, on websites, etc.); limiting the offering of daily redemptions (exchanges/fund platforms can play an important role in this regard); and by ensuring they are adequately managing liquidity risk, e.g. by increasing the share of liquid assets and possibly applying liquidity management tools such as swing pricing.

Banks

As advisors and dealers, banks can: encourage issuers to obtain a credit rating and discourage the issuance of a large number of smaller bonds; publish price data in a timely manner (including for private placements); and finally possibly enter into resale agreements whereby issuers pay them to be more active in the markets, although the report notes that this may also bring disadvantages such as increased borrowing costs, since the pricing of such services may be difficult.

Note: [1] The value reduction of the fund as a share of its current value in a scenario where the interest rate spread between its holdings and government bonds doubles.
Source: Riksbanken (2021[41]), Towards a better functioning corporate bond market, https://www.riksbank.se/globalassets/media/rapporter/riksbanksstudie/engelska/2021/towards-a-better-functioning-corporate-bond-market.pdf.

2.9. The role of real estate companies in the Swedish corporate bond market

The real estate sector represents an important part of the Swedish corporate bond market, accounting for almost half of total outstanding bonds issued in domestic currency by amount (Wollert, 2020[13]). This has raised concerns that a fall in real estate prices could reverberate through other sectors of the corporate bond market, threatening financial stability more generally (Riksbanken, 2021[41]). This is particularly relevant given the very steep increase in property valuations in Sweden since the mid-1990s, and has been further exacerbated by the sharp increases in interest rates since 2022. Work within the OECD Capital Market Series typically does not include the real estate sector. However, given the size, concentration and importance of real estate companies in the Swedish bond market, this section provides an overview of the sector's use of corporate bond financing and how it compares to that of other non-financial companies. The Annex provides details on the types of companies that are included in this analysis.

Real estate companies have gone from representing a negligible share of the Swedish bond market to becoming very substantial, accounting for 37%[18] of outstanding amounts at the end of 2023. In 2021, they represented as much as 48% of total issuance (Figure 2.24, Panels A and B).[19] Issuance has been particularly high since 2017, averaging USD 10.8 billion annually between 2017 and 2021, up from an average of USD 3.3 billion from 2010 to 2016. However, because the real estate industry is typically very interest rate-sensitive, issuance contracted 66% in 2022, down to representing 29% of total issuance. Issuance contracted by another 11% in 2023.

Figure 2.24. The real estate sector's role in the Swedish corporate bond market

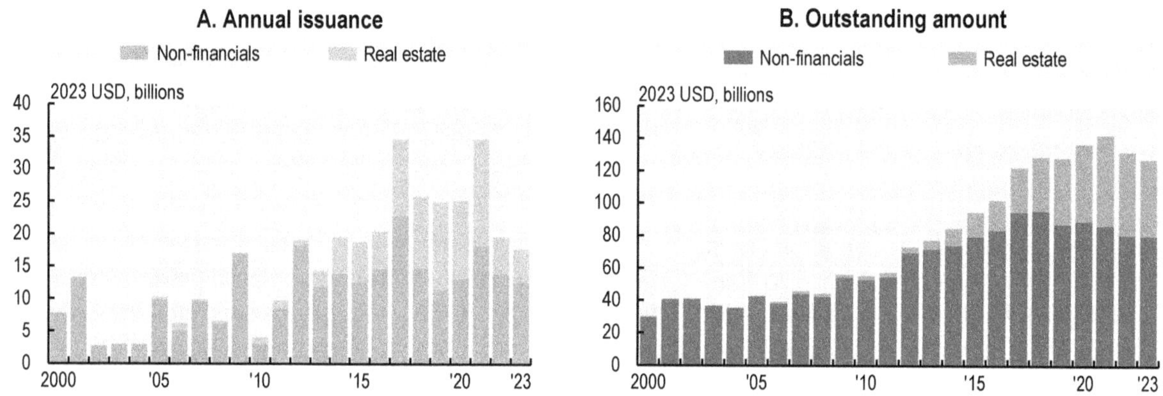

Source: OECD Capital Market Series dataset, LSEG, see Annex for details.

Including real estate companies in the analysis significantly changes the industry composition shown in Figure 2.13. As shown in Figure 2.25, between 2019 and 2021 real estate companies made up roughly half of annual issuance, up from 20% on average between 2010 and 2015. This degree of concentration exposes the bond market as a whole to fluctuations within the dominant industry. Given the real estate sector's particularly strong link to the financial sector (e.g. because of the amount of real estate collateral held by banks), this lack of diversification may be a financial stability concern, especially when considering the prospect of longer periods of stricter financial conditions and its likely impact on real estate prices. A protracted downturn could impact the two main sources of credit, the banking sector and the bond market, simultaneously. The impact of tighter credit conditions on the sector can be seen in 2022 and 2023, when its share in total issuance decreased sharply.

It bears noting that real estate companies do not seem to issue foreign currency denominated bonds to a greater extent than non-financial companies. In fact, they have issued a larger share of SEK-denominated bonds in the last decade.

Figure 2.25. Industry composition of the Swedish corporate bond market (% of amount issued)

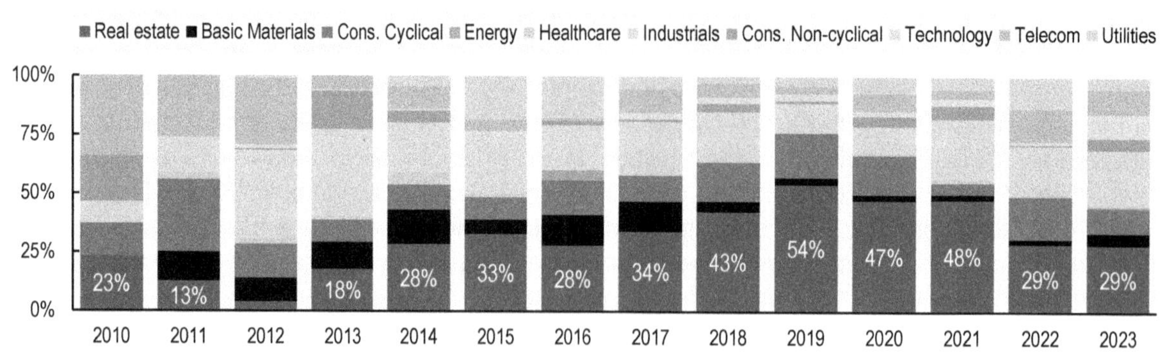

Source: OECD Capital Market Series dataset, LSEG, see Annex for details.

The median issue size by real estate companies has remained relatively constant since 2012, averaging USD 49 million between 2012 and 2023 (Figure 2.26, Panel A). The distribution of issue sizes is weighted more towards smaller issues among real estate companies than is the case for the broader non-financial universe. While the two smallest size categories (below USD 100 million) made up 71% of the total number of issues by non-financial companies in 2023, for real estate companies it was as high as 96%. In spite of this, the concentration of total issue amounts by the top ten real estate issuers is higher than for non-financial companies (Figure 2.26, Panels A and B). The top three real estate companies have represented an average of 41% of total issuance by the sector in the past five years, compared to 35% for the top three non-financial companies. This is partly a natural effect of a smaller sample of real estate companies, but it is also because many of the largest real estate companies issue several smaller bonds in any given year rather than issuing fewer, but larger bonds. This can be seen when comparing the share of the three largest bonds in total issuance in a year with the share of the total amount issued by the three largest issuers. For example, between 2015 and 2023, the three largest real estate bonds made up an average of 18% of total issuance annually. However, the three largest issuers made up an average of 43% of annual issuance, meaning their total issuance is made up by a set of smaller bonds.

This happens because companies want to issue bonds with different profiles (e.g. with respect to maturities to smooth their repayment schedule or in different currencies to attract different investors) and is not limited to the real estate sector. However, Swedish real estate companies issue a larger number of bonds per issuer than non-financial companies do. Between 2015 and 2023, non-financial companies (those issuing bonds) issued an average of 2.2 bonds per year. The corresponding figure for real estate companies was twice as high at 4.4 bonds per issuer and year, indicating it is composed of active issuers to a greater extent than the broader non-financial group. Similarly, when looking at the median issue size (the bond) as a percentage of the median issuer size (the company) between 2015 and 2022, the average figure for real estate companies is lower (1.4%) than for non-financial companies (1.7%), meaning the former group of companies tends to issue smaller individual bonds relative to their size.

Figure 2.26. Size distribution and concentration of real estate issuers

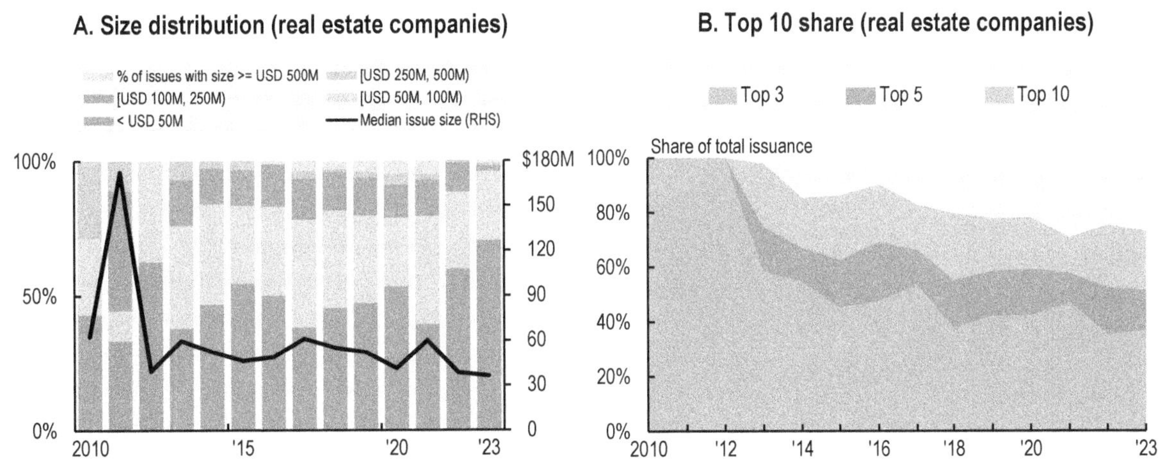

Source: OECD Capital Market Series dataset, LSEG, see Annex for details.

The real estate sector has generally converged with the non-financial sector over time both in terms of credit ratings and maturity profile, although there was some divergence in 2022. In 2021, the value-weighted average maturity of real estate bonds was 7.8 years, compared to 8.4 years for the non-financial sector. In 2022, however, the average maturity decreased sharply to 4.7 in the real estate sector years whereas in the non-financial sector it increased to 9.5 years. In 2023, maturities for the non-financial sector decreased to 6 years and for real estate remained similar to that in 2022 (Figure 2.27, Panel A). As noted in section 2.3, when considering equal-weighted averages, maturities are shorter. This also holds for real estate companies, for which the simple average maturity in 2023 was only 3.9 years. The median was as low as 3.0 years.

The groups were even closer in terms of credit ratings in 2021, with the average value-weighted rating for real estate company bonds at 12.4 (about half a notch above BBB-) compared to 12.3 for non-financial companies. In 2022, the average rating for real estate companies increased much more sharply, to 15.7, than that of non-financial companies (13.3). The two converged somewhat again in 2023. These developments are likely an effect of the particular difficulties faced by the real estate sector in a context of increased remote work and rising interest rates, leaving primarily higher-rated companies with (affordable) access to funding. Historically, the real estate sector had substantially higher ratings than the non-financial sector, in the order of three full notches on average between 2013 to 2016 (real estate company bonds had an average rating corresponding to A, compared to BBB for non-financial company bonds) (Figure 2.27, Panel B).

Figure 2.27. Maturity and credit rating profile of the real estate sector

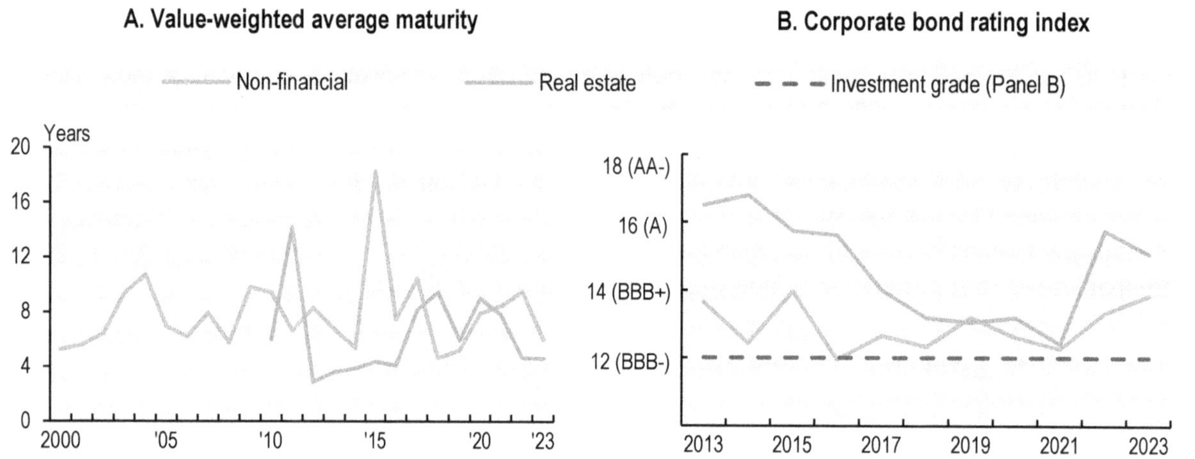

Note: The real estate time series starts in 2010 in Panel A because issuance before that year was very small. The same applies for rated bonds in Panel B (from 2013). The peak for non-financial companies in 2015 in Panel A is driven by a set of four large bonds (between USD 344 million to USD 1.05 billion) issued by state-owned power company Vattenfall with maturities between 62 and 63 years. See Figure 2.6 for equal-weighted maturities.

3 The Swedish corporate bond market in an international comparison

This chapter puts the Swedish corporate bond market in an international context, comparing it with selected European and non-European markets. It also discusses some of the regulatory aspects that affect the secondary corporate bond market and its functioning, such as transparency rules in trading and pricing.

This chapter provides a comparison of the Swedish market with a number of countries/regions with respect to both the primary and secondary markets. The quantitative analysis in this section does not include real estate companies.

3.1. Market size and characteristics

Testament to the sharp growth in Swedish bond markets, since 2005 the share of debt securities in non-financial companies' total financial debt has grown faster in Sweden than in any of the other regions shown below. Between 2005 and 2019, the share increased by 61% in Sweden, compared to 15% in the United Kingdom, 12% in the United States and 32% in the Euro Area (Figure 3.1, Panel A). The share dropped somewhat thereafter but recovered in 2023. As a result of this growth, Sweden now has a higher share of debt securities in total financial debt than the euro area aggregate. At the end of the second quarter of 2023 it was 16%, compared to 11% in the euro area and 20% in the United Kingdom. In the United States, the share of debt securities in total financial debt was 60% (Panel B).

Figure 3.1. Debt securities, share in total financial debt

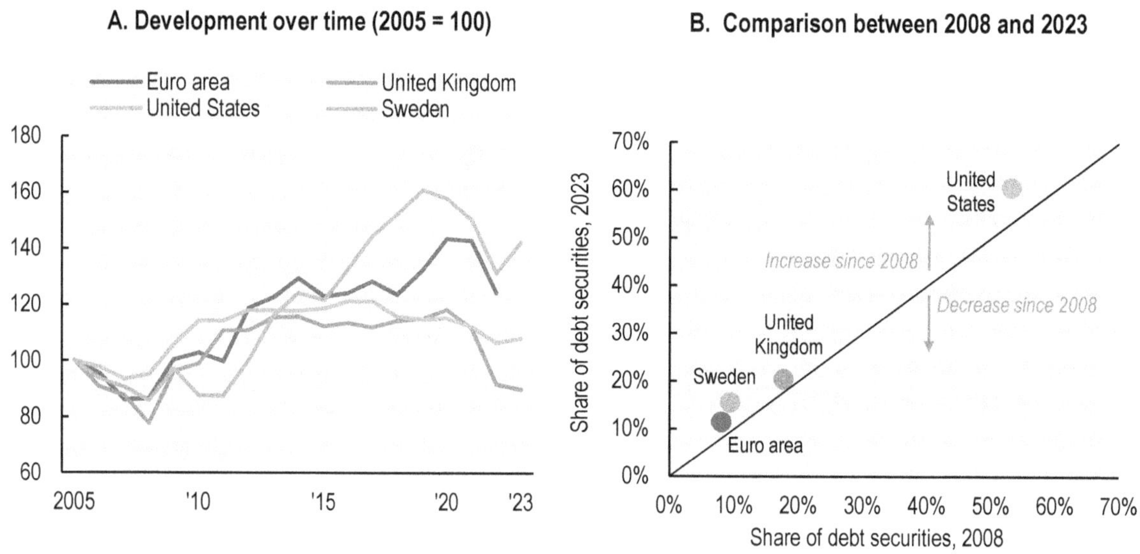

Note: Panel A shows the share of debt securities (long-term and short-term) in total debt financing (the sum of total loans and total debt securities) for non-financial companies. 2023 data as of Q2-2023. Data for the euro area are for Q4-2022.
Source: ECB; Swedish Financial Accounts from Statistics Sweden (SCB); UK Office for National Statistics; US Federal Reserve.

Sweden has the largest non-financial corporate bond market in the Nordics. At the end of 2023, the total outstanding amount was USD 80 billion, equivalent to 14% of GDP, slightly higher than in Norway (13% of GDP), and much higher than in Denmark (8% of GDP) and Finland (10% of GDP). However, it is still significantly smaller than certain European peers, notably the Netherlands, where the total outstanding amount represents 52% of GDP (Figure 3.2, Panel A).

The Swedish market's development over time differs from many other countries. Panel B below shows how the number of issuers and median issue size have changed between the periods 2010-15 and 2016-23 (averages for both periods). A movement upwards (downwards) indicates an increase (decrease) in the number of issuers, whereas a move to the left (right) indicates a decrease (increase) in the median issue size. Notably, Sweden has moved upwards to the left, almost doubling the number of unique issuers while decreasing the median issue size by more than 60%. As mentioned when discussing Figure 2.11, this shows how the market has expanded to include a larger number of smaller companies. In fact, in 2021

Sweden had more issuers than the much larger Dutch market. Norway has followed a similar trajectory. Contrarily, in the Netherlands both the number of issuers and the median issue size have increased. The Danish and Finnish markets remain limited in size, with no more than 7 and 12 issuers in 2023, respectively.

Figure 3.2. Non-financial corporate bond markets, international comparison

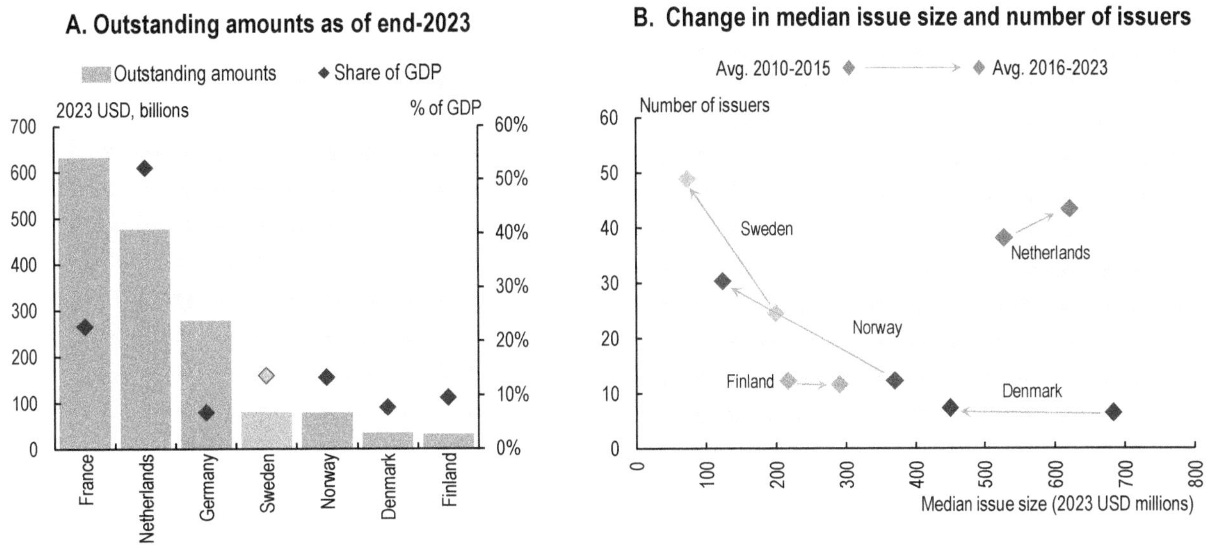

Source: OECD Capital Market Series dataset, LSEG, see Annex for details.

The industry composition of corporate bond issues in Sweden has changed, as shown in Figure 2.13, and the degree of concentration has increased somewhat. As shown in Figure 3.3, the dominant industry changed (from utilities to industrials) between 2000-11 and 2012-23, and the share of the top industry in total issuance increased from 29% to 34%.[20] This level of concentration places Sweden at the higher end among its peers. Norway has the highest degree of concentration, with the energy sector representing 50% (63%) of total issuance in 2012-23 (2000-11). In the past decade, the countries with the lowest industry concentration were the Netherlands and the United States, both with consumer cyclicals at 18% and 17% respectively (Panel B).

Figure 3.3. Industry concentration, total non-financial issuance (not including real estate)

Source: OECD Capital Market Series dataset, LSEG, see Annex for details.

Looking at the share of the top ten issuers in total issuance offers another measure of market concentration as well as an indication of how the market has changed over time. Figure 3.4 below provides an international comparison of how that share changed from 2005-2015 to 2016-2023. Concentration decreased in seven out of the eight countries/regions shown below, by an average of 11%. Concentration increased marginally in the United States (although from a much lower level than the other countries). In Sweden the decrease was as much as 27 percentage points, indicating the extent to which the market has broadened. Its concentration is now slightly less than the EU average.

Figure 3.4. Top ten issuers' share in total issuance

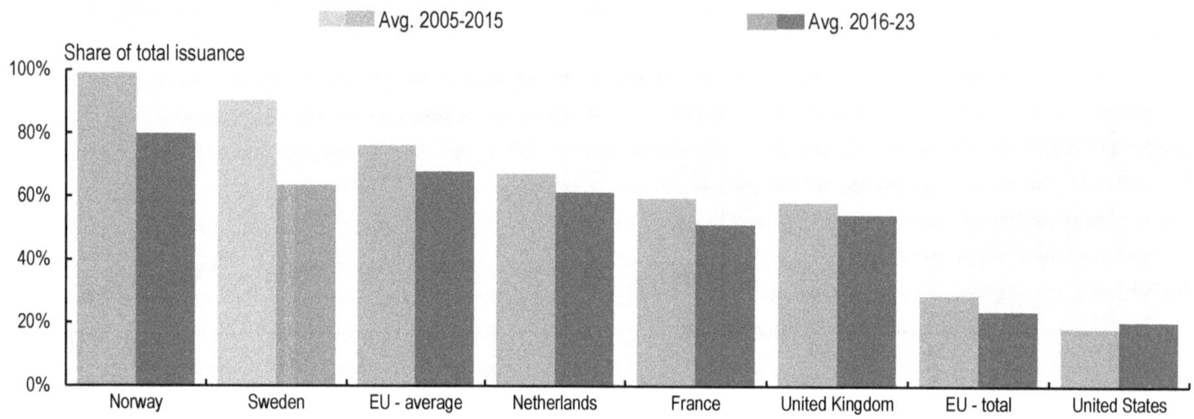

Note: "EU – average" refers to the weighted average of the EU27; it is calculated by adding up the top 10 issuers' total issuance in each EU country in each year and then dividing that sum by the total issuance in the EU. "EU – total" refers to the share of the 10 largest issuers in the EU as a whole.
Source: OECD Capital Market Series dataset, LSEG, see Annex for details.

Many companies are active internationally and have revenues in several different currencies, making foreign currency borrowing a useful tool for matching payments and revenues and reducing exchange rate risk exposure. It may also be a strategy for obtaining lower financing costs, as illustrated by the fact that between 2015 and 2017, when US and euro area interest rates diverged as the Federal Reserve began tightening monetarily policy while the ECB maintained an expansionary position, US companies issued record levels of euro-denominated debt (8% of total issuance during the period) (Çelik, Demirtaş and Isaksson, 2019[44]).

Panel A in Figure 3.5 below shows the share of domestic currency issuance since 2010 in different regions. The increase in domestic currency issuance in Sweden earlier shown in Figure 2.7 is clearly visible. Unsurprisingly, companies in the United States (94% in 2023) and the EU (81%) predominantly finance themselves with domestic currency denominated debt, given their globally dominant currencies and the significant size of their internal markets. In 2023, 53% of Swedish non-financial bonds by amount were issued in the domestic currency, higher than companies in the United Kingdom (which issue significant amounts in both EUR and USD).

Panel B shows the average foreign currency-denominated issue size between 2010-23 as a multiple of the average domestic-currency issue size across countries. A higher multiple indicates a larger difference between average amounts raised in foreign currency and domestic currency issues. As expected, smaller countries with smaller domestic corporate bond markets show higher multiples, suggesting that large companies that issue in foreign markets issue relatively larger amounts compared to those issuing domestically. In Sweden, the average foreign-currency denominated bond is 3.9 times larger than the average SEK-denominated bond. In Norway, which has a smaller non-financial corporate bond market than Sweden but some very large companies (notably in the energy sector), the multiple is as high as 5.8x.

Figure 3.5. Foreign/domestic currency issuance across regions

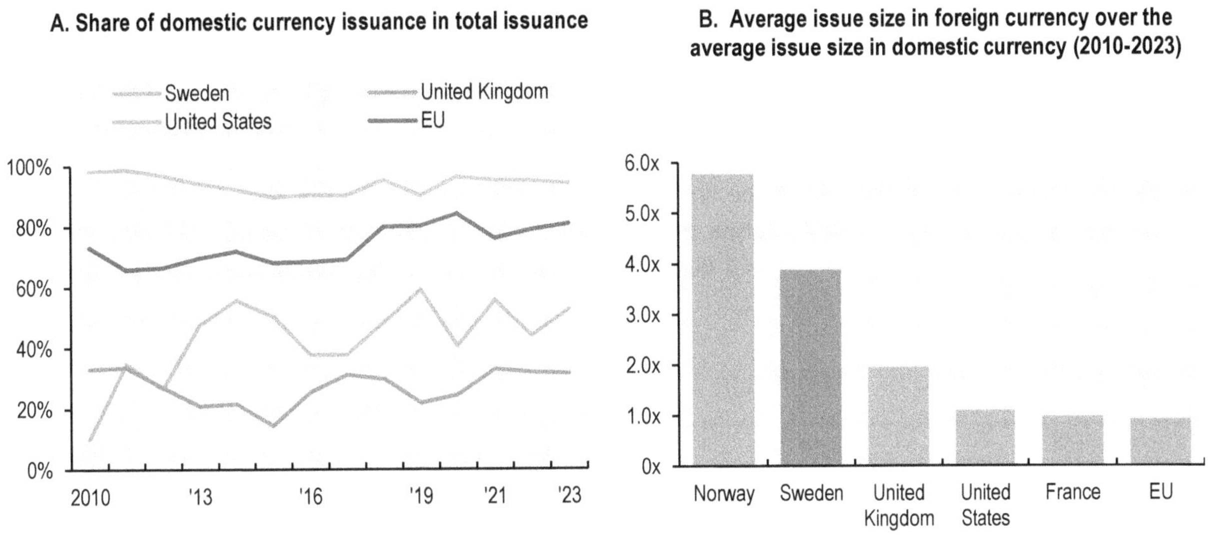

Note: Foreign currency issuance within the EU could for example be an EU country outside of the euro zone issuing a bond in euros.
Source: OECD Capital Market Series dataset, LSEG, see Annex for details.

As discussed in Chapter 2 (and shown in Figure 2.3), Sweden has a high share of bonds without credit ratings (even when including local ratings). Figure 3.6 compares this share with those in other countries. In terms of amounts, Sweden had the third highest share of unrated bonds among the countries below in the period from 2000 to 2023. At 21% of aggregate issuance, it is lower than in Finland and Norway but 3.5 times higher than the share in France and almost six times higher than the share in the Netherlands. The figures are similar when looking at the number of unrated bonds instead (which is generally higher since larger issues are more likely to have credit ratings). Unrated issuers in Sweden include smaller companies as well as large, well-known companies (Wollert, 2020[13]).

Figure 3.6. Share of unrated corporate bonds in total non-financial issuance, 2000-23

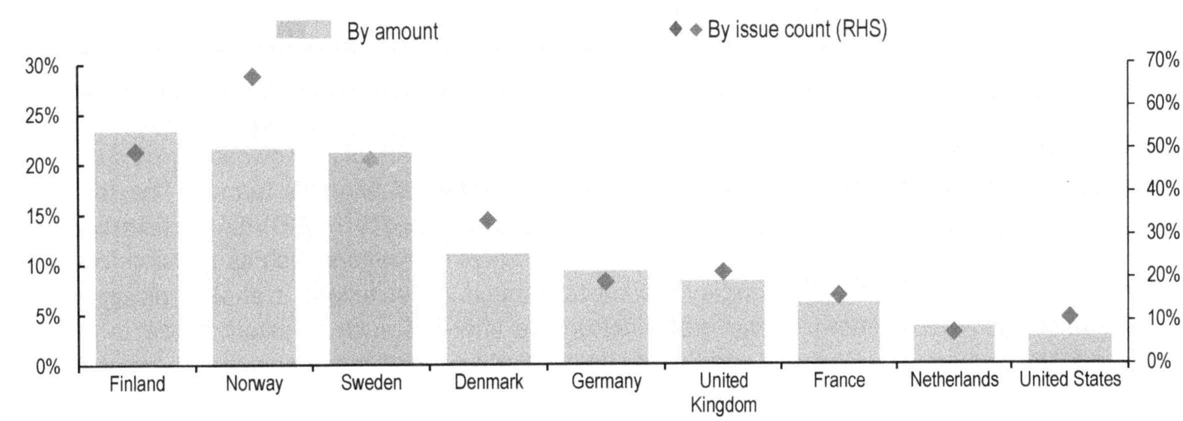

Note: Refers to bonds not rated by either S&P, Moody's or Fitch. As illustrated in Figure 2.4, including local ratings has a negligible impact.
Source: OECD Capital Market Series dataset, LSEG, see Annex for details.

Issuing a bond involves a number of costs that can be significant to smaller companies. The issuance cost varies across regions. For example, in the United States the cost is estimated to be around 0.6% of the total proceeds, whereas in Europe the median cost is approximately 0.4% (OECD, 2017[45]). In addition to the fees paid to the underwriting bank and other advisors as well as the cost of obtaining a credit rating, listing the bonds on an exchange involves listing fees. Table 3.1 below provides a comparison of the fees charged by the four most common exchanges used by Swedish non-financial companies that list their bonds: Nasdaq Stockholm, Luxembourg, London and Dublin (see also Figure 2.8). The figures are calculated for two different principal amounts, EUR 50 million and EUR 500 million, and assumes a five-year maturity. All fees refer to the full five-year period. Notably, the Stockholm exchange has no registration fees, only annual maintenance fees. The opposite model applies on the London Stock Exchange, which only charges fees at the time of listing but not afterwards. For both a smaller bond with a face value of EUR 50 million and a larger one of EUR 500 million, the Luxembourg exchange charges the lowest fees, although the differences are relatively small, especially compared to the London and Stockholm exchanges.

Table 3.1. Cost of listing a bond with a maturity of five years, by exchange

EUR	Stockholm	Luxembourg	London	Dublin
		Principal: EUR 50m		
Approval fee (one-off)	-	3 000	2 320	8 500
Listing fee (one-off)	-	1 500	6 699	540
Maintenance fee (annual)	9 962	2500	-	16 500
Total (5 years)	**9 962**	**7 000**	**9 019**	**25 540**
		Principal: EUR 500m		
Approval fee (one-off)	-	3 000	2 320	8 500
Listing fee (one-off)	-	1 500	6 960	540
Maintenance fee (annual)	9 962	3500	-	16 500
Total (5 years)	**9 962**	**8 000**	**9 280**	**25 540**

Note: As of October 2023. Assumes listing on the Standard/Regulated Tier of each market. Includes approval fees paid to regulators. Excludes VAT. Maturity is assumed to be five years, and costs refer to the full cost over that period. It is assumed that it is the issuer's first bond listing – discounts are sometimes given for subsequent listings. For Euronext Dublin, the approval fee includes: Euronext Document Fee and Central Bank of Ireland Document Fee, while the listing fee refers to the formal notice fee.
Source: Nasdaq Stockholm, Bourse de Luxembourg, London Stock Exchange and Euronext Dublin.

As noted in Section 2.5, investment funds make up a substantial share of domestic ownership of Swedish corporate bonds. Figure 3.7 below shows that the holdings of investment funds are also higher than in some other countries, most notably Denmark, the Netherlands and France. That can have financial stability implications. Investment funds, most notably open-ended funds, need to trade actively in the secondary market in response to fund in- and outflows. Open-ended corporate bond funds effectively offer short-term liquidity based on a portfolio of mostly illiquid instruments. When the share of total ownership by such funds is high, it can expose the market to significant pressure in times of financial turmoil. The regulatory measures taken with respect to investment fund redemptions in response to the COVID-19 crisis discussed under section 2.8.2 seek to mitigate that risk. Contrarily, long-term investors such as pension funds and insurance companies trade in the secondary market to a much lesser extent, if at all, typically holding bonds to maturity. As also shown in the graph below, the share of such investors is low in Sweden compared to the Netherlands, Denmark and France. In the Netherlands, for example, the share of pension and insurance fund ownership is two and a half times higher than in Sweden. However, while long-term investors tend to offer more stability, the tool through which they do so – holding until maturity – has detrimental impacts on secondary market liquidity. That does not necessarily imply that the reverse is true: having a large share of investors that need to be active in secondary market trading does not necessarily create more liquidity. If active secondary market investors' demand is highly correlated (for example selling in a downturn in response to increased redemptions), the market will be one-sided, with no beneficial effects on liquidity. Indeed, the fact that Sweden has a high share of investment fund investors does not seem to have had any significant positive impact on secondary market liquidity.

It is worth noting that increasing ownership of corporate bonds by open-ended funds is a global trend. Over the past ten years, the exposure to corporate bonds by open-ended funds and exchange traded funds have increased substantially (OECD, 2024[24]).

Figure 3.7. Domestic ownership of non-financial corporate bonds by investor type, Q2-2023

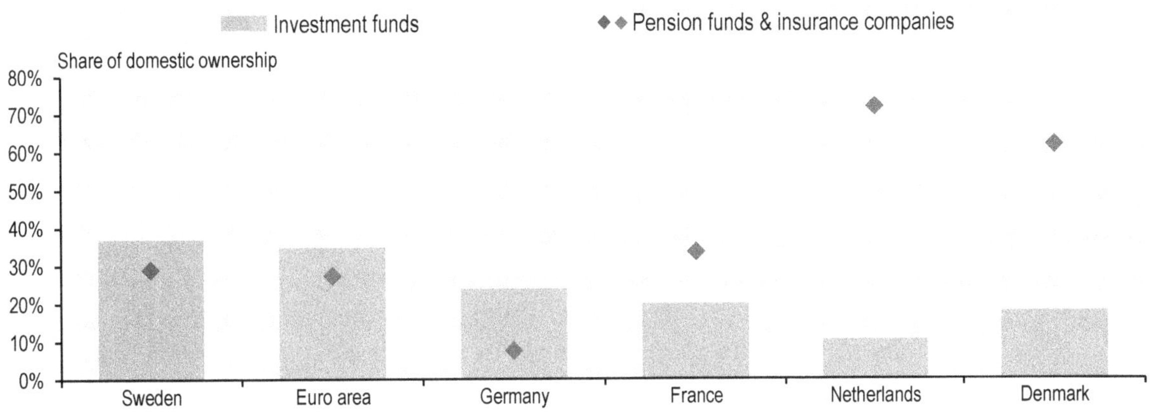

Note: Data for the euro area refer to Q4-2022.
Source: ECB.

3.2. Transparency and disclosure rules for corporate bond trading

An important aspect of the functioning of a corporate bond market is the rules that apply with respect to transparency and disclosure. These affect the liquidity and price discovery mechanism of the market as well as investor confidence. Transparency rules, when functioning properly, can also help regulators detect potential misconduct and unfair pricing. However, a balance needs to be struck to ensure adequate transparency without discouraging dealer intermediation, in particular for illiquid bonds. As discussed under section 2.8, the waivers applicable under the existing MiFIR/D II framework actually led to a decrease in transparency in the Swedish bond market. To put the Swedish and European frameworks into context, this section offers an international comparison of how transparency and disclosure rules apply on other bond markets, notably in the United States.

Since different rules typically apply depending on the listing status of a bond, it is useful to first clarify the terminology used. Table 3.2 below provides a summary of the terminology applied, which is in line with IOSCO (2017[46]). Note that, according to the IOSCO definitions, a bond that is only admitted to trading on a non-exchange trading venue such as an alternative trading system (ATS), an organised trading facility (OTF) or, most notably in Sweden, a multi-lateral trading facility (MTF), is considered *unlisted*, which may differ from the national understanding of what it means to be "listed".

There are substantial cross-country differences in transparency and reporting requirements, both in terms of design and application. In addition, there are differences with respect to pre- and post-trade transparency rules (as mentioned in Chapter 2, due to waivers in MiFIR/D II, all investment firms trading in Swedish bonds are exempt from pre-trade disclosure). For example, for regulatory reasons, most corporate bonds in the EU are listed, while trading is primarily done OTC. However, under MiFIR/D II transparency rules apply based on listing status rather than mode of trading, meaning that any trade – including OTC – in a listed bond is subject to the rules under the MiFIR/D II framework. In the United States and Canada, where most bonds are unlisted and traded OTC, there are elaborate transparency rules applicable to trading in these securities. Listed bonds usually have to comply with the rules set by the exchange on which they are listed (IOSCO, 2017[46]).

Table 3.2. Terminology – bond types

Status	Description	Possible trading venues
Listed	Bonds listed or admitted to trading on a regulated exchange.	• Regulated exchange • Non-exchange trading venues (e.g. ATS, MTF or OTF) • OTC
Unlisted	Any bond not listed on a regulated exchange. Includes bonds admitted to non-exchange trading venues.	• Non-exchange trading venues (e.g. ATS, MTF or OTF) • OTC

Source: IOSCO (2017[46]), Regulatory Reporting and Public Transparency in the Secondary Corporate Bond Markets, https://www.iosco.org/library/pubdocs/pdf/IOSCOPD578.pdf.

The United States has a well-developed system for OTC trading called the *Trade Reporting and Compliance Engine* (TRACE), which has been in place since 2002. TRACE is operated by the Financial Industry Regulatory Authority (FINRA), a self-regulatory organisation authorised by the US Congress to oversee broker-dealer operations.[21] All broker-dealer member firms are obliged to report OTC transactions in TRACE-eligible securities under rules approved by the Securities and Exchange Commission (SEC) (FINRA[47]). Through this system, prices and trade volumes are disseminated to market participants in near real time for OTC trading. In addition to intra-day data, the system also provides aggregate trading statistics (e.g. most active bonds, total volume traded, etc.) at the end of each day (at 19.00 Eastern Time). As discussed above, due to the nature of the instrument, the impact of increased transparency on the liquidity of corporate bond markets is not entirely clear-cut. For this reason, TRACE was phased in gradually, allowing for a continuous study of its effect on liquidity. In the first years, the reporting window was successively shortened from 75 minutes after a transaction was completed, down to within 15 minutes since early January 2006. The scope of securities was also gradually expanded, initially including primarily large (USD 1 billion or above) bonds with high credit ratings. By early 2005, it had been expanded to cover 99% of all public transactions in eligible securities. After a transaction has been reported, it is immediately disseminated through TRACE. These data are then accessible through all major data vendors and to retail investors on the FINRA website (CFA Institute, 2011[48]). In 2024, FINRA proposed an amendment to further reduce the reporting delay to one minute (US SEC, 2024[49]).

Contrary to some expectations, TRACE has not led to a greater concentration in dealers (see discussion on dealer incentives under section 2.8). Dealer activity has instead remained rather high and no significant detrimental effects on dealer-provided liquidity have been observed. More generally, a meta-study of the effect of transparency on liquidity (including other markets and systems than the US and TRACE), found that a majority of studies indicated that higher transparency is at least somewhat beneficial (CFA Institute, 2011[48]).

As discussed in Section 2.8, despite the intentions of MiFIR/D II regulations to increase transparency in the corporate bond market, the waivers included have *de facto* had the opposite effect. This experience is not unique to the Swedish market; in a 2019 survey on MiFID II the International Capital Market Association (ICMA) found that a number of challenges remained to be addressed, most notably a continued lack of post-trade transparency even two years after the implementation of the new rules. The report also points out that certain rules on the primary market have led to greater administrative burdens for companies without much benefit, in particular the allocation justification recording (where firms providing placing services to issuers need to keep an audit trail, a non-public written record of the justification for each investor allocation made). Several respondents also indicated that it is difficult to identify whether a counterparty is a systematic internaliser (SI), an investment firm that on a frequent, systematic and substantial basis executes client orders on its own account, outside of trading venues, which is important to know since it has implications for the post-trade reporting requirements for OTC transactions. Finally, the ICMA report highlights the difficulty of accessing post-trade data published through Approved Publication Arrangements (APAs), and the fact that many respondent firms consider the vast majority of such data to be unusable due to low quality. However, it bears mentioning that while 60% of respondents in 2019 said price discovery had not improved following the implementation of MiFIR/D II, this was a decrease from 70% in 2018 and almost a third said it had improved somewhat. Further, the regulation has likely been a driver of the observed increase in electronic trade flows (ICMA, 2019[50]). It remains to be seen what the impact of the MiFIR review proposals will be.

In order to contextualise the transparency and disclosure framework in Sweden and the EU, Table 3.3 below provides a comparison between the reporting delays applied under the MiFIR/D II framework and those that apply in a selected number of peer countries, drawing from a comparative study conducted by IOSCO (2017[46]). The table shows how the rules apply depending on 1) the trading venue (exchange, non-exchange trading venue or OTC) and 2) whether disclosure is pre- or post-trading. Rules for listed and unlisted bonds (in line with the definition given in Table 3.2) are shown separately. The symbols used are explained in the notes to the table.

It should be noted that while the table shows that the EU rules require near real-time transparency both pre- and post-trade, numerous waivers significantly affect how these rules work in practice, in particular in smaller markets where liquidity is low, as discussed in Section 2.8. As the table illustrates, many jurisdictions make data available for listed bonds in real-time to the public only against a fee, releasing it for free after a delay (often 15-20 minutes). Self-regulatory organisations play an important role in several markets, notably in the United States (FINRA), Korea (KOIFA) and Canada (IIROC), as well as in Japan (JSDA, not shown below).

With respect to the primary market, an important part of the bond issuance process is the allocation of bonds. In order to find a consensus price, the lead manager(s) (the bank(s) mandated to manage the issuance process) will seek to gather a sufficiently large number of possible investors. Consequently, bond issues are often oversubscribed. In response to this, certain investors will inflate their orders to receive a larger share of bonds in the allocation process, to the detriment of investors that are constrained by internal rules forbidding them to place orders in excess of what they actually want to invest. The allocation is supposed to be carried out according to rules agreed with the issuer, and lead managers are to keep records of the process. However, the process tends to be less transparent for high-yield bonds (European Commission, 2017[51]). Under the European Union's MiFIR/D II framework, firms providing placing services to issuers are obliged to keep an audit trail justifying each investor allocation.

Table 3.3. Regulatory reporting in selected jurisdictions

Listed bonds										
	Trading venue									
	Exchange				Non-exchange trading venue				OTC	
	Pre-trade: real time disclosure to...		Post-trade: real-time disclosure to...		Pre-trade: real time disclosure to...		Post-trade: real-time disclosure to...		Dissemination	
	Exchange users	**Public**	**Exchange users**	**Public**	**Exchange users**	**Public**	**Exchange users**	**Public**	**Pre-trade**	**Post-trade**
Australia	✓	✓ $	✓	✓ $ (20 min)	n/a*	n/a*	n/a*	n/a*	Operates under exchange markets, so real-time just like on exchange	
Canada	✓	✓ $	✓	✓ $	✓	✓ $	✓	✓ $	n/a	
Korea	✓	✓	✓	✓ $	n/a	n/a	n/a	n/a	Self-regulatory organisation and information vendors	

Listed bonds										
Sweden/EU	✓	✓	✓	✓	✓	✓	✓	✓	SIs must make public firm quotes, subject to conditions	Through APAs for bonds admitted to trading
Switzerland	✓	✓$ (15 min)	✓	✓$ (15 min)	×	×	× (T+3)	× (T+3)	Exchange Market Data Systems, Market, Data Vendors, Internet	
United States	✓	✓	✓	✓$	Depends**	×	15 min	15 min	TRACE system (FINRA)	

Unlisted bonds						
	Trading venue					
	Non-exchange trading venue				OTC	
	Pre-trade data available to ...		Post-trade data available		Dissemination	
	Exchange	**Public**	**Exchange**	**Public**	**Pre-trade**	**Post-trade**
Australia	n/a	n/a	n/a	n/a	n/a	Summary information by trade association
Canada	✓***	×	✓	✓	n/a	T+2 by self-regulatory organisation
Korea	n/a	n/a	n/a	n/a	✓	Within 15 mins by self-regulatory association
Sweden/EU	✓ (Continuous basis)	✓ (Continuous basis)	✓ (Real-time/close to)	✓ (Real-time/close to)	SIs must make public firm quotes, subject to conditions	Through APAs for bonds admitted to trading
Switzerland	n/a	n/a	n/a	n/a	n/a	n/a
United States					TRACE system (FINRA)	

Note: For listed bonds, real-time data are often made available to the public against a fee. This is indicated by the ✓$ symbol. Cases where the information is available in real-time for a fee, but made publicly available for free after a certain time period are indicated by ✓$ (x min), where the brackets indicate the delay before information is made available for free. The table does not reflect the EU's MiFIR review proposals.

* Australia has no alternative market license framework.

** Available in real time if the venue in question maintains an order book or displays quotations.

*** Displayed to users in real time if in an order book and otherwise displayed.

Source: IOSCO (2017[46]), Regulatory Reporting and Public Transparency in the Secondary Corporate Bond Markets, https://www.iosco.org/library/pubdocs/pdf/IOSCOPD578.pdf.

References

Abudym, M. and A. Wohl (2018), "Corporate Bond Trading on a Limit Order Book Exchange", *Review of Finance*, pp. 1413-1440, https://doi.org/10.1093/rof/rfx054. [36]

Bao, J., J. Pan and J. Wang (2011), "The Illiquidity of Corporate Bonds", *Journal of Finance*, https://doi.org/10.1111/j.1540-6261.2011.01655.x. [18]

BCS (2016), "GUÍA DEL MERCADO DE DEUDA BURSÁTIL", https://servicioscms.bolsadesantiago.com/Corporativo/Documentos/20160913%20Gu%C3%ADa%20del%20Mercado%20de%20Deuda%20Burs%C3%A1til.pdf. [38]

BCS (n.d.), *Montos Transados*, https://www.bolsadesantiago.com/estadisticas_montostransados (accessed on 2023). [39]

Becker, B. et al. (2020), *Kan obligationsmarknaden dämpa kreditcykeln?*, Finansinspektionen, https://www.fi.se/contentassets/787944581b974c2a81d97797d50e665b/fi-analys-23-obligationsmarknaden-n.pdf. [26]

Bessembinder, H. and W. Maxwell (2008), "Transparency and the Corporate Bond Market", *Journal of Economic Perspectives*, https://doi.org/10.1257/jep.22.2.217. [11]

Bessembinder, H., C. Spatt and K. Venkataraman (2020), "A Survey of the Microstructure of Fixed-Income Markets", *Journal of Financial and Quantitative Analysis*, Vol. 55/1, pp. 1-45, https://doi.org/10.1017/S0022109019000231. [31]

Brugler, J., C. Comerton-Forde and J. Martin (2022), "Secondary Market Transparency and Corporate Bond Issuing Costs", *Review of Finance*, https://doi.org/10.1093/rof/rfab017. [12]

Çelik, S., G. Demirtaş and M. Isaksson (2019), *Corporate Bond Markets in a Time of Unconventional Monetary Policy*, OECD Capital Market Series, Paris, http://www.oecd.org/corporate/Corporate-Bond-Markets-in-a-Time-of-Unconventional-Monetary-Policy.htm. [44]

Çelik, S., G. Demirtaş and M. Isaksson (2015), *Corporate Bonds, Bondholders and Corporate Governance*, OECD Corporate Governance Working Papers No. 16, https://doi.org/10.1787/5js69lj4hvnw-en. [30]

CFA Institute (2011), "An Examination of Transparency in European Bond Markets", https://www.cfainstitute.org/-/media/documents/article/position-paper/an-examination-of-transparency-in-european-bond-markets.ashx. [48]

Chen, L., D. Lesmond and J. Wei (2007), "Corporate Yield Spreads and Bond Liquidity", *Journal of Finance*, https://doi.org/10.1111/j.1540-6261.2007.01203.x. [17]

Confederation of Swedish Enterprise (2012), *Letter from the Confederation to the Ministry of Finance on August 9, 2012: Begäran om förtydliganden i lagstiftningen rörande agentrollen vid emissioner av företagsobligationer m.m.* [5]

Edwards, A., E. Lawrence and M. Piwowar (2007), "Corporate Bond Market Transaction Costs and Transparency", *The Journal of Finance*, https://doi.org/10.1111/j.1540-6261.2007.01240.x. [9]

ESMA (2021), *EU Securities Markets: ESMA Annual Statistical Report 2021*, https://www.esma.europa.eu/sites/default/files/library/esma50-165-2004_eu_securities_markets_asr_2021.pdf. [33]

ESMA (2018), *ESMA Fines Five Banks €2.48 Million For Issuing Credit Ratings Without Authorisation*, https://www.esma.europa.eu/press-news/esma-news/esma-fines-five-banks-%E2%82%AC248-million-issuing-credit-ratings-without-authorisation. [7]

ESRB (2019), *EU Non-bank Financial Intermediation Risk Monitor 2019*, https://www.esrb.europa.eu/pub/pdf/reports/nbfi_monitor/esrb.report190717_NBFImonitor2019~ba7c155135.en.pdf. [42]

Eurofi (2023), *Summary - Eurofi High Level Seminar, Stockholm April 2023*, pp. 25-28, https://www.eurofi.net/wp-content/uploads/2023/07/summary_the-eurofi-high-level-seminar_stockholm_april-2023.pdf. [20]

European Commission (2023), *Commission welcomes political agreement on the review of the Markets in Financial Instruments Regulation*, https://finance.ec.europa.eu/news/commission-welcomes-political-agreement-review-markets-financial-instruments-regulation-2023-06-30_en. [8]

European Commission (2017), *Improving European corporate bond markets - Report from the Commission Expert Group on Corporate Bonds*, https://ec.europa.eu/info/sites/default/files/171120-corporate-bonds-report_en.pdf. [51]

European Parliament and the Council of the European Union (2014), *Regulation (EU) No 596/2014 of the European Parliament and of the Council of 16 April 2014 on market abuse (market abuse regulation)*, https://eur-lex.europa.eu/legal-content/EN/TXT/?uri=celex%3A32014R0596. [4]

Finansinspektionen (2023), *Inside information*, https://www.fi.se/en/markets/issuers/inside-information/. [53]

Finansinspektionen (2022), *Dags för en svensk benchmarkstandard för företagsobligationer*, https://www.fi.se/sv/publicerat/tal-och-debatt/2022/dags-for-en-svensk-benchmarkstandard-for-foretagsobligationer/. [15]

Finansinspektionen (2021), *Debattartikel i Dagens Industri 9/6: Obligationsmarknaden måste ha högre likviditet*, https://www.fi.se/sv/publicerat/tal-och-debatt/2021/debattartikel-i-dagens-industri-18-3-obligationsmarknaden-maste-ha-hogre-likviditet/. [14]

Finansinspektionen (2021), *Konsekvenser av ett utsträckt prospektansvar för juridiska personer*, https://www.fi.se/contentassets/59296ae182334feebecefde05ab155be/konsekevenser-prospektansvar-juridiska-personer.pdf. [1]

Finansinspektionen (2021), *Liquidity tools in UCITS and special funds (Swe. Likviditetsverktyg i värdepappersfonder och specialfonder)*, https://www.fi.se/contentassets/48de81a2cd08467a91fa8606f7f52076/likviditetsverktyg-vardepappersfonder-specialfondern3.pdf. [43]

Finansinspektionen (2019), *New rules led to reduced transparency on the Swedish bond markets*, No. 15, https://www.fi.se/contentassets/0174249373f1415bb14bd2bd14a77307/fi-tillsyn-15-transparens-obligationsm-engn.pdf. [34]

FINRA (n.d.), *Trade Reporting and Compliance Engine (TRACE)*, https://www.finra.org/filing-reporting/trace. [47]

FSB (2021), *The behaviour of dealers in corporate bond markets in March 2020.* [27]

Goldstein, M., E. Hotchkiss and E. Sirri (2007), "Transparency and Liquidity: A Controlled Experiment on Corporate Bonds", *The Review of Financial Studies*, https://doi.org/10.1093/rfs/hhl020. [10]

ICMA (2022), *Secondary Market Practices Committee: European Secondary Bond Market Data*, https://www.icmagroup.org/assets/SMPC-Secondary-Market-Bond-Data-H2-2022.pdf. [32]

ICMA (2019), *MiFID II/R and the bond markets: the second year*, https://www.icmagroup.org/assets/documents/Regulatory/MiFID-Review/MiFID-II-R-and-the-bond-markerts-the-second-year-201219.pdf. [50]

IOSCO (2017), "Regulatory Reporting and Public Transparency in the Secondary Corporate Bond Markets", https://www.iosco.org/library/pubdocs/pdf/IOSCOPD578.pdf. [46]

Lidman, E. (2023), "Finns det en värdepappersmarknadsrättlig princip om likabehandling av obligationsinnehavare?", *Juridisk tidskrift*, pp. 786-809. [3]

Lidman, E. (2020), *Kontrollägande och uppköpsreglering*, Swedish Corporate Governance Forum. [52]

Li, J. and H. Yu (2022), "Investor Concentration, Liquidity and Bond Price Dynamics", https://doi.org/10.2139/ssrn.4083526. [19]

Longstaff, F., S. Mithal and E. Neis (2005), "Corporate Yield Spreads: Default Risk or Liquidity? New Evidence from the Credit Default Swap Market", *The Journal of Finance*, https://doi.org/10.1111/j.1540-6261.2005.00797.x. [16]

Mizrach, B. (2015), "Analysis of Corporate Bond Liquidity", *FINRA Office of the Chief Economist, Research Note*, https://www.finra.org/sites/default/files/OCE_researchnote_liquidity_2015_12.pdf. [29]

Nordic Trustee (2020), *Corporate Bond Market Report*, https://nordictrustee.com/app/uploads/2021/02/NordicTrustee_CorporateBondMarketReport_2020.pdf. [25]

OECD (2024), *Global Debt Report 2024: Bond Markets in a High-Debt Environment*, OECD Publishing, https://doi.org/10.1787/91844ea2-en. [24]

OECD (2021), *The Future of Corporate Governance in Capital Markets Following the COVID-19 Crisis*, https://doi.org/10.1787/efb2013c-en. [6]

OECD (2020), *OECD Capital Market Review of Portugal 2020: Mobilising Portuguese Capital Markets for Investment and Growth*, OECD Capital Market Series, https://www.oecd.org/corporate/ca/OECD-Capital-Market-Review-Portugal-2020.pdf. [22]

OECD (2019), *Equity Market Review of Asia 2019*, OECD Capital Market Series, Paris, https://www.oecd.org/corporate/ca/OECD-Equity-Market-Review-Asia-2019.pdf. [28]

OECD (2017), *OECD Business and Finance Outlook, Chapter 2 - Globalisation and the level playing field*, https://doi.org/10.1787/9789264274891-en. [45]

Riksbanken (2021), *Towards a better functioning corporate bond market*, https://www.riksbank.se/globalassets/media/rapporter/riksbanksstudie/engelska/2021/towards-a-better-functioning-corporate-bond-market.pdf. [41]

Riksbanken (2014), *The development of the Swedish market for corporate bonds*, http://archive.riksbank.se/Documents/Rapporter/Ekonomiska_kommentarer/2014/rap_ek_kom_nr07_141015_eng.pdf. [21]

Swedish Securities Markets Association (2020), *The Swedish Securities Markets Association contributes to increased transparency on the bond market*, https://svenskvardepappersmarknad.se/wp-content/uploads/2020/11/SSMA-Press-Release-Bond-Market-Transparency-24-Nov-2020.pdf. [35]

TASE (2022), *Trading Statistics*, https://info.tase.co.il/Eng/Statistics/TradingStatistics/TradeGuide6A/Pages/table6A.aspx?Action=4&issubmitted=1. [37]

TASE (n.d.), *Trading Statistics*, https://market.tase.co.il/en/market_data/monthly-review/securities?dType=1 (accessed on 2023). [40]

The Swedish Stock Market Self-Regulation Committee (2021), *Takeover rules for Nasdaq Stockholm and Nordic Growth Market NGM*, https://regelkommitten.se/userfiles/pdfer/rules_english/takeover_rules/Takeover_rules_2021-01-01.pdf. [2]

US SEC (2024), *Release No. 34-99404; File No. SR-FINRA-2024-004:*, https://www.sec.gov/files/rules/sro/finra/2024/34-99404.pdf. [49]

VVF (2023), *Verdipapirfondenes forenings bransjestandard for informasjon og klassifisering av rentefond*, https://vff.no/documents/Bransjenormer/Bransjestandarder/Bransjestandard-for-informasjon-og-klassifisering-av-rentefond-vedtatt-23.-mars-2023.pdf. [23]

Wollert, S. (2020), *Swedish corporate bonds during the coronavirus pandemic*, Riksbanken, https://www.riksbank.se/globalassets/media/rapporter/staff-memo/engelska/2020/swedish-corporate-bonds-during-the-coronavirus-pandemic.pdf. [13]

Annex A. Methodology for data collection and classification

Corporate bond data

Information presented on corporate bond issuances are based on OECD calculations using international deal-level data on new issues of corporate bonds that are underwritten by an investment bank, obtained from LSEG. The database provides a detailed set of information for each corporate bond issue, including the identity, nationality and sector of the issuer; the type, interest rate structure, maturity date and rating category of the bond, the amount of and use of proceeds obtained from the issue.

Convertible bonds, deals that were registered but not consummated, preferred shares, sukuk bonds, bonds with an original maturity less than or equal to one year or an issue size less than USD 1 million are excluded from the dataset. The analyses in the report are limited to bond issues by non-financial companies. The industry classification is carried out based on LSEG's business classification TRBC. First-level industry groups (TRBC Economic Sector) are used for all analyses except for those involving real estate companies. These companies are included in the financials first-level group, so a second-level industry group (TRBC Industry Group) is used to identify them. Only companies classified as active within real estate operations are included. REITs are excluded. The country breakdown is carried out based on the issuer's country of domicile. Yearly issuance amounts initially collected in USD were adjusted by 2023 US Consumer Price Index (CPI). Information provided in monthly frequency is collected and presented in current USD.

Given that a significant portion of bonds are issued internationally, it is not possible to assign such issues to a certain country of issue. For this reason, the country breakdown is carried out based on the country of domicile of the issuer.

Rating data

LSEG provides rating information from three leading rating agencies: S&P, Moody's and Fitch. Each bond that has rating information available in the dataset is assigned a value between 1 (lowest, C) and 21 (highest, AAA for S&P and Fitch and Aaa for Moody's). There are 11 non-investment grade categories: five from C (C to CCC+); and six from B (B- to BB+). There are ten investment grade categories: three from B (BBB- to BBB+); and seven from A (A- to AAA).

If ratings from multiple rating agencies are available for a given issue, their average is used. Some issues in the dataset, on the other hand, do not have rating information available. For such issues, the average rating of all bonds issued by the same issuer in the same year (t) is assigned. If the issuer has no rated bonds in year t, year t-1 and year t-2 are also considered, respectively. This procedure increases the number of rated bonds in the dataset and hence improves the representativeness of rating-based analyses. When differentiating between investment and non-investment grade bonds, the final rating is rounded to the closest integer and issues with a rounded rating less than or equal to 11 are classified as non-investment grade.

Early redemption data

When calculating the outstanding amount of corporate bonds in a given year, issues that are no longer outstanding due to being redeemed earlier than their maturity should also be deducted. The early redemption data are obtained from LSEG and cover bonds that have been redeemed early due to being repaid via final default distribution, called, liquidated, put or repurchased. The early redemption data are merged with the primary corporate bond market data via international securities identification numbers (ISINs).

Covenant data

Covenant data are collected from LSEG. The LSEG screen provides different flags indicating whether or not the instrument in question includes a certain type of covenant. The below flags were collected for all available Swedish bonds. Their descriptions, as provided by LSEG, are included.

- *Collective Action Clauses flag:* A y/n flag indicating whether the bond carries Collective Action Clauses (examples: LATAM global issues or Model CAC introduced on 1 January 2013 for all Eurozone government bond issuance).
- *Force Majeure flag:* A y/n flag indicating if the parties are freed from their obligations in the event of an act of God (flooding, hurricanes, etc.). For example, if the Issuer loses all of their assets in an earthquake rendering them unable to pay back investors.
- *Negative Pledge flag:* A y/n flag indicating that the Issuer would not issue another bond of the same type in the future that would have a higher priority in case the Issuer defaults.
- *Sale Leaseback flag:* A y/n flag where a 'y' means the issuer may not, and may not permit any (restricted) subsidiary to, enter into any sale and leaseback transaction, subject to exceptions.
- *Change of Control Put flag:* A y/n flag indicating whether there is a provision in the indenture or agreement that allows investors to put the asset, if there are specified changes in ownership control of the entity responsible for the servicing of the debt.
- *Pari Passu flag:* A y/n flag indicating that a debt instrument carries the same degree of ranking without any preference among other debt securities with similar ranking.
- *Merger flag:* A y/n flag indicating where 'y' would mean that the issuer may not consolidate or merge with or wind up into, or sell, assign, transfer, lease, convey or otherwise dispose of all or substantially all of its properties or assets in one or more related transactions, to any person or entities.
- *Default Events flag:* A y/n flag indicating if offering the document of the debt instrument contains events that constitute 'events of defaults'.
- *Sale of Assets flag:* A y/n flag indicating if the issuer is prohibited from sale of assets which would cause the issuer to cease to exist or which could reduce the creditworthiness of the issuer.
- *Keepwell Agreement flag:* A y/n flag indicating if the instrument is backed by a keep-well agreement between the issuer and another entity, most often the parent of the issuer. A keep-well agreement is not an explicit guarantee, but benefits from the agreement provider in case of insolvency of the issuer.
- *Cross Default flag:* A y/n flag indicating if the issuer or guarantor or parent defaults on any of its debt instruments and the default continues beyond the grace period, then such event shall constitute a default on all of its debt instruments, which have equal priority of payment.
- *Debt Incurrence Limitation flag:* A y/n flag where 'y' means the issuer will not, and will not permit any of its (restricted) subsidiaries to incur any indebtedness except permitted indebtedness, if any.

Consultations

During the spring of 2022, the OECD carried out fact-finding missions where the team conducted consultations with representatives of both government institutions and market participants, including the Swedish Riksbank, the Swedish Financial Supervisory Authority (*Finansinspektionen*), Nasdaq Stockholm, leading legal and financial advisors, as well as investors, banks, issuers and agents (in total around 40 experts). In addition, following the initial interviews, a number of in-depth interviews have been carried out with investors and intermediaries to better understand developments, strengths and weaknesses of the Swedish corporate bond market. These consultations have benefited the report greatly, and the team gratefully acknowledges the participants' important contributions.

Notes on data updates in this report

Figure 2.18 and Figure 2.22: In a previous mapping report of the Swedish corporate bond market dating from October 2022 (*The Swedish Corporate Bond Market and Bondholder Rights*) these figures included trading with the issuer of the security (primary market). These trades have been excluded in the present version. For further information related to SELMA fixed income statistics, refer to the Swedish Riksbank's *Statistical definitions for the fixed income market (FI) reporting*, https://www.riksbank.se/globalassets/media/statistik/selma/2016/new-fi_definitions.pdf.

Figure 2.19: Since the publication of the above-mentioned report, Statistics Sweden has updated its financial accounts for Sweden, significantly revising the data with respect to net credit flows. The figure and the corresponding text commentary have been updated to reflect this change.

Notes

[1] See Directive 2004/25/EC on takeover bids, Article 3(1)(a) which is repeated in the introduction to the Stock Market Self-Regulation Committee's takeover rules for both regulated markets and trading platforms as well as in point II.10.

[2] Sometimes called "the Swedish Takeover Panel". See in particular points II.11-16 of the Takeover Rules. The Swedish Securities Council has addressed the issue of equal treatment of target company shareholders in a significant number of statements (Lidman, 2020[52]).

[3] On many markets, a "trustee" will be appointed for a bond issuance, with a legal position determined under the law of trusts. Anglo-Saxon trust law is not recognised under Swedish law. Instead, a similar, but not identical, legal figure is created through the bond term contracts. This legal figure is described as an "agent", which is the term applied in this report. This should however be distinguished from the legal figure sometimes described as a "paying agent", which also appears in international bonds, but which has a significantly more limited role than an "agent" under Swedish law.

[4] Now Nordic Trustee – the main independent agent on the Swedish market.

[5] See the Finnish Act 25.8.2017/574 on representatives of bondholders and the Danish regulation on "representative" in Danish law LBK nr 1 229 af 07 September 2016. For Norwegian law, see e.g. *Høyesteretten*'s judgements HR-2010-00568-A and HR-2010-01489-U.

[6] See also the proposal for the Finnish Act for a comprehensive discussion of the role and position of the agent, proposal RP 48/2017 vp.

[7] These figures are based on transactions involving US companies.

[8] There were a number of sizeable domestic currency denominated bonds issued in 2007 and 2008, notably by manufacturing company Scania and state-owned power company Vattenfall.

[9] Notable USD denominated issues (>USD 500 million) without listing include Ellevio (2016), Atlas Copco (2007) and Stena (2014).

[10] In practice, the incentives of the trustee to conduct any significant covenant compliance due diligence are rather weak, owing to a fixed fee structure and potential professional liability concerns. Their tasks are therefore often limited to administrative procedures. See e.g. (Çelik, Demirtaş and Isaksson, 2015[30]) for a more thorough review.

[11] See Finish law 25.8.2017/574, and the regulation pertaining to the "repræsentant" in Danish law LBK nr 1 229 af 07 September 2016.

[12] These requirements normally do not apply to investment firms trading only bilaterally. However, for so-called systematic internalisers (executing orders against their own books), it is mandatory to quote bids and offers. Such trading has increased since 2018, with corresponding reductions in OTC trading.

[13] The survey includes market participants dealing in government bonds and covered bonds, in addition to corporate bonds.

[14] An OTF is an Organised Trading Facility. MiFID II introduced OTFs as a new trading venue category, a multilateral system in which multiple third-party buying and selling interests in bonds, structured finance product, emissions allowances or derivatives are able to interact. An OTF is neither a regulated market nor a multilateral trading facility (MTF).

[15] Defined as a low-volume investor with less than NIS 2 million (USD 559 000) in all TASE securities excluding options.

[16] April and September: Verisure; June: Ellevio (two bonds); September: Volvo Cars.

[17] The FSA calls this "adjusted sale and redemption price", a method whereby the price of the fund units is adjusted up or down depending on net flows. Another type of swing pricing, which it calls "adjusted net asset value", involves adjusting the value of the fund, which is not allowed in current fund-related legislation.

[18] This share differs from that shown in the central bank's staff memo (Wollert, 2020[13]). This is this is due to the following differences in methodology: 1) the central bank's figures refer only to outstanding bonds issued in the domestic currency, while the present report also includes bond issued in foreign currency; and 2) possible differences in the industry classification used.

[19] Throughout this subsection, "total issuance/outstanding amounts" refer to the sum of issuance/outstanding bonds by non-financial companies and real estate companies.

[20] When including real estate companies in this analysis, that becomes the dominant sector in Sweden from 2011-21, but the top issuer's share in total issuance does not change in any significant way. The top industry does not change for any other country.

[21] FINRA was previously known as the National Association of Securities Dealers (NASD).

www.ingramcontent.com/pod-product-compliance
Lightning Source LLC
Chambersburg PA
CBHW061225240926
51846CB00006B/1357
* 9 7 8 9 2 6 4 9 3 7 9 2 5 *